THE CAMPER CONVERSION MANUAL™

How to convert Volkswagen

BUS
or VAN
to CAMPER

D1519114

First published in 2004. Veloce Publishing Ltd., 33 Trinity Street, Dorchester DT1 1TT, England. Fax 01305 268864. E-mail: veloce@veloce.co.uk. Web: www.veloce.co.uk
ISBN 1-903706-45-9/UPC 36847-00245-9

Readers with ideas for automotive books, or books on other transport or related hobby subjects, are invited to write to the editorial director of Veloce Publishing at the above address.

British Library Cataloguing in Publication Data -
A catalogue record for this book is available from the British Library.
Typesetting, design and page make-up all by Veloce on Apple Mac.
Printed in Italy.

THE CAMPER CONVERSION MANUAL™

How to convert Volkswagen

BUS
VAN
or
to CAMPER

Lindsay Porter

VELOCE PUBLISHING
THE PUBLISHER OF FINE AUTOMOTIVE BOOKS

Contents

Introduction & acknowledgements

Safety First!

When most people think of camper vans, they invariably think of Volkswagens. In fact, it's arguable that VW started the camper van trend in the early 1950s when the first of the Type 2s (the type number given to all Transporters, initially to distinguish them from Type 1 Beetles), were converted and used in that first flush of post-war freedom from conflict in Europe.

Cut to today and there's still no substitute for the reliability and practicality of a VW Camper conversion, even though things have moved on considerably from those early days. The first Transporter, the split-screen model, now called T1 by Volkswagen, and its successor, the 'Bay Window' (T2) model are very much sought after and cared for. They're not covered in this manual, though, simply because the raw materials, in the form of bare vans waiting to be converted, are not readily available. Type 2 T3s, built from 1980 to 1991 and Type 2 T4s, built from 1991-on, can still be found earning their keep as working vans and there are even versions available with factory-fitted side windows. T3s (rear-engined) and T4s (front-engined) are also available with various petrol/gasoline engine sizes as well as in diesel and/or 4WD Syncro form, and often with other mod cons, such as power steering, electric windows and mirrors,

Intro 1. A pair of camper conversions which you'll find featured throughout this manual.

air conditioning, central locking and excellent heaters!

There are several VW Camper converters around, many of them carrying out top-class work. Why, then, has just one of those VW-approved converters, Leisuredrive of Manchester, been singled out for the 'big treatment' in this manual? The reason is quite simple. Right from the start, Leisuredrive's proprietor, Derek Andrews, threw himself into this project with great enthusiasm. Over a period of years, his commitment and that of his staff has been consistent and unwavering.

I dread to think what my presence at the Leisuredrive factory must have cost them in real terms as a result of the time I spent poking my nose and my camera lens (it just about sticks out further than my nose), into their work, and I hope that the sincere comments I have made throughout this book about the honest workmanship I found there are useful to them. There's another reason for featuring Leisuredrive. As well as carrying out large numbers of conversions, the company is prepared to sell you the components to allow you to do all or part of the conversion work yourself,

Intro 4. The all-new VW T5 van and MPV range, introduced in 2003/4 (depending on version), is larger than the outgoing T4 range and was regarded as a leap forward in van design and dynamics at launch.

Intro 3. T2 'Bay Window' campers can still be found providing plodding, pedestrian but persevering service. For the pedants, it's known by VW as a T2, Volkswagen Type 2.

Intro 2. Just as the first VW van - always designated Type 2 to distinguish it from the Beetle's 'Type 1' nomenclature - was the first of its type, the 'split screen' (now known as T1), Camper is the model that started off the whole camper van scene.

depending on the extent of your ambition and ability. The usual approach is to have Leisuredrive fit the roof and windows for you and then to fit out the interior yourself. Of course, you could do it all if you're sufficiently competent.

Other specialists have also thrown their weight behind this manual and they can be found listed in Chapter 7. It's true

to say that, without their help, this project would not have been possible.

Finally, my grateful thanks are due to Shan, my wife, whose unflagging support makes possible this whole strange business of my being a motoring writer, and to my assistant, Zoe Palmer, without whose organisational skills and practical knowledge this book would surely never have been finished, and certainly not half as well as I hope it has.

SAFETY FIRST!

You must always ensure that safety is the first consideration in any job you carry out. A slight lapse in concentration, or a rush to finish the job quickly can easily result in an accident, as can failure to follow the precautions outlined here. Whereas skilled motor mechanics are trained in safe working practices you, the home mechanic, must find them out for yourself.

Remember, accidents don't just happen, they are caused, and some of those causes are contained in the following list. Above all, ensure that whenever you work on your vehicle you adopt a safety-minded approach at all times, and remain aware of the dangers that might be encountered.

Be sure to consult the suppliers of any materials and equipment you may use, and obtain and read carefully any operating and health and safety instructions that may be available on packaging or from manufacturers and suppliers.

PART I: IMPORTANT POINTS
Vehicle off ground
• **Always** ensure that the vehicle is properly supported when raised off the ground. Don't work on, around, or underneath a raised vehicle unless axle stands or hoist lifting pads are positioned under secure, load bearing underbody

Safety 1. Always ensure that the safe working load rating of any jacks, hoists or lifting gear used is sufficient for the job, and that lifting gear is used only as recommended by the manufacturer.

areas. If the vehicle is driven onto ramps, the wheels remaining on the ground must be securely chocked to prevent movement.
• **Never** work on a vehicle supported only by a jack.
• **Never** attempt to loosen or tighten nuts that require a lot of force to turn (e.g. a tight oil drain plug), with the vehicle raised,

Safety 2. Axle stands also need to be up to the job. These inexpensive Clarke stands have an SWL of 3 tonnes. Make sure that the axle stands will each be placed beneath a reinforced part of the body, suitable for jacking from, or a main suspension mounting. Never place the axle stand under a moving suspension part.

Safety 3. DON'T lean over, or work on, a running engine unless it is strictly necessary, and keep long hair and loose clothing well out of the way of moving mechanical parts. Note that it is theoretically possible for fluorescent striplighting to make an engine fan appear to be stationary - double check whether it is spinning or not! This is the sort of error that happens when you're really tired and not thinking straight.

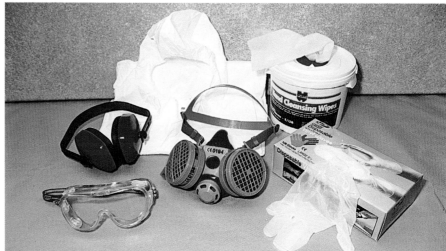

Safety 4. Wurth produces a huge range of workshop products, including the safety-related items shown here.

unless it is safely supported. Take care not to pull the vehicle off its supports when applying force to any part of the vehicle. Wherever possible, initially slacken tight fastenings before raising the vehicle off the ground.
• **Always** wear eye protection when working under the vehicle and when using power tools.

Using trolley jack and axle stands
On many occasions, you will need to raise the vehicle with a trolley jack - invest in one if you don't already own one. Ensure that the floor is sufficiently clear and smooth for the trolley jack wheels to roll as the vehicle is raised and lowered, otherwise it could slip off the jack.
• Before raising the vehicle, **ensure that the handbrake (parking brake) is off and the gearbox is in neutral**. This is so that the vehicle can move as the jack is raised.
• Reapply the parking brake and put the vehicle in gear after raising is complete. Chock each wheel to prevent vehicle movement.
• Remember to release the parking brake, put the gearbox in neutral and remove the chocks before lowering the vehicle again.
• Whenever you're working beneath a vehicle, have someone keep an eye on you!
• If someone pops out to see how you are getting on at regular intervals, it could be

enough to save your life!

Working on the vehicle
• **Always** seek specialist advice unless you are justifiably confident about carrying out each job. The safety of your vehicle affects you, your passengers, and other road users.
• **Don't** work on your vehicle when you're overtired.
• **Always** work in a well ventilated area and don't inhale dust - it may contain asbestos or other harmful substances.
• Remove your wrist watch, rings and all other jewellery before doing any work on the vehicle - and especially when working on the electrical system.
• **Don't** remove the radiator or expansion tank filler cap when the cooling system is hot, or you may get scalded by escaping coolant or steam. Let the system cool down first, and even then, if the engine is not completely cold, cover the cap with a cloth and gradually release the pressure.
• **Never** drain oil, coolant or automatic transmission fluid when the engine is hot. Allow time for it to cool sufficiently to avoid scalding you.
• **Always** keep antifreeze, brake and clutch fluid away from vehicle paintwork. Wash off any spills immediately.
• Take care to avoid touching any engine or exhaust system component unless it's cool enough not to burn you.

Running the vehicle
• **Never** start the engine unless the gearbox is in neutral (or 'Park' in the case of automatic transmission), and the

handbrake is fully applied.
• **Never** run catalytic converter-equipped vehicles without the exhaust system heat shields in place.
• Take care when parking vehicles fitted with catalytic converters. The 'cat' reaches extremely high temperatures and any combustible materials under the vehicle, such as long dry grass, could be ignited.

Personal safety
• **Never** siphon fuel, antifreeze, brake fluid or other potentially harmful liquids by mouth, or allow contact with your skin. There is an increasing awareness that they can damage your health. Best of all, use a suitable hand pump and wear gloves.
• Before undertaking dirty jobs, use a barrier cream on your hands as a protection against infection. Preferably, wear impervious gloves - disposable types are ideal - where there is a risk of used engine oil or any other harmful substance coming into contact with your skin.
• Wipe up any spilt oil, grease or water off the floor immediately, before there is an accident.
• Make sure that spanners/wrenches and all other tools are the right size for the job and are not likely to slip. Never try to 'double-up' spanners to gain more leverage.
• Seek help if you need to lift something heavy which may be beyond your capability. Don't forget that when lifting a heavy weight, you should keep your back straight and bend your knees to avoid injuring your back.
• **Never** take risky short-cuts or rush to

Safety 5. There are several types of fire extinguisher. Take advice from your accredited supplier to make sure that you have the right type for workshop use. Note that water fire extinguishers are not suitable for workshop or automotive use.

Safety 6. Avoid the use of mains electricity when working on the vehicle whenever possible. For instance, you could use rechargeable tools and a DC inspection lamp, powered from a remote 12V battery - both are much safer. However, if you do use mains-powered equipment, ensure that the appliance is wired correctly to its plug, that where necessary it is properly earthed (grounded), and that the fuse is of the correct rating for the appliance. For instance, a 13 amp fuse in a lead lamp's plug will not provide adequate protection. Do not use any mains-powered equipment in damp conditions or in the vicinity of fuel, fuel vapour or the vehicle battery.

finish a job. Plan ahead and allow plenty of time.
• Be meticulous and keep the work area tidy - you'll avoid frustration, work better and lose less.
• Keep children and animals well away from the work area and from unattended vehicles.
• **Always** tell someone what you're doing and have them regularly check that all is well, especially when working alone on, or under, the vehicle.

PART II: HAZARDS
Fire!
• Petrol (gasoline) is a dangerous and highly flammable liquid requiring special precautions. When working on the fuel system, disconnect the vehicle battery earth (ground) terminal whenever possible and always work outside, or in a very well ventilated area. Any form of spark, such as that caused by an electrical fault, by two metal surfaces striking against each other, by a central heating boiler in the garage 'firing up', or even by static electricity built up in your clothing can, in a confined space, ignite petrol vapour causing an explosion. Take great care not to spill petrol onto the engine or exhaust system, never allow a naked flame anywhere near the work area and, above all, don't smoke!

Pressure
• Don't disconnect any fuel pipes on a fuel injected engine while the ignition is switched on. The fuel in the line is under very high pressure - sufficient to cause serious injury. Remember that many

injection systems have residual pressure in the pipes for days after switching off. Consult the workshop manual or seek specialist advice before carrying out any work.

Fumes
• In addition to the fire dangers described previously, petrol (gasoline) vapour and the types of vapour given off by many solvents, thinners and adhesives are highly toxic and, under certain conditions, can lead to unconsciousness or even death if inhaled. The risks are increased if such fluids are used in a confined space, so always ensure adequate ventilation when handling materials of this nature. Treat all such substances with care, always read the instructions and follow them with care.
• Always ensure that the vehicle is out of doors and not in an enclosed space when the engine is running. Exhaust fumes contain poisonous carbon monoxide, even when the vehicle is fitted with a catalytic converter, since 'cats' sometimes fail and don't function when the engine is cold.
• Never drain petrol (gasoline) or use solvents, thinners, adhesives or other toxic substances in an inspection pit as the extremely confined space allows the highly toxic fumes to concentrate. Running the

engine with the vehicle over the pit can have the same results. It is also dangerous to park a vehicle for any length of time over an inspection pit. The fumes from even a slight fuel leak can cause an explosion when the engine is started. Petrol fumes are heavier than air and will accumulate in the pit.

Mains electricity
Before using any mains-powered electrical equipment, take one more simple precaution - use an RCD (Residual Current Device) circuit breaker. Then, if there is a short circuit, the RCD circuit breaker minimises the risk of electrocution by instantly cutting the power supply. Buy one from any electrical store or DIY centre. RCDs fit simply into your electrical socket before plugging in your electrical equipment.

The ignition system
• Touching certain parts of the ignition system, such as the HT leads, distributor cap, ignition coil, *etc.*, can result in a severe electric shock. This is especially likely where the insulation on any of these components is weak, or if the components are dirty or damp. Note also that voltages produced by electronic ignition systems are much higher than those produced by conventional systems and could prove fatal, particularly to people with cardiac pacemaker implants. Consult your handbook or main dealer if in any doubt.
• An additional risk of injury can arise while working on running engines whereby

Safety 7. Never work on the ignition system with the ignition switched on, or with the engine being turned over on the starter, or running.

a shock could cause the operator to pull his or her hand away on to a sharp, conductive or revolving part.

The battery

• Battery terminals on the vehicle should be shielded, since a spark can be caused by any metal object which touches the battery's terminals or exposed connecting straps.

• Before working on the fuel or electrical systems, always disconnect the battery earth (ground) terminal.

• Before charging the battery from an external source, disconnect both battery leads before connecting the charger. If the battery is not of the 'sealed-for-life' type, loosen the filler plugs or remove the cover before charging. For best results the battery should be given a low rate trickle charge overnight. Do not charge at an excessive rate or the battery may burst.

• Always wear gloves and goggles when carrying or when topping up the battery.

Safety 8. When using a battery charger, care should be taken to avoid causing a spark by switching off the power supply before the battery charger leads are connected or disconnected. This is what can happen to a leisure battery when a spark came into contact with it - with the battery caps properly fitted! A spark can enter one of the vent holes causing the battery to explode and throw acid a surprising distance. Keep a stored battery well away from work areas.

Safety 9. Never smoke, cause a spark, or allow a naked light near the vehicle's battery, even in a well ventilated area. A certain amount of highly explosive hydrogen gas will be given off as part of the normal charging process.

Even in diluted form (as it is in the battery), the acid electrolyte is extremely corrosive and must not be allowed to contact the eyes, skin or clothes.

Brakes and asbestos

• Obviously, a vehicle's brakes are among its most important safety-related items. **Only** work on your vehicle's braking system if you are trained and competent to do so, **unless** you have someone who is a trained mechanic thoroughly check and approve your work, and your vehicle's braking system as a whole, before the vehicle is used on the road.

• Whenever you work on the braking system's mechanical components, or remove front or rear brake pads or shoes: i) wear an efficient particle mask; ii) wipe off all brake dust from the work area after spraying on a proprietary brand of brake cleaner (never blow dust off with compressed air); iii) dispose of brake dust and discarded shoes or pads in a sealed plastic bag; iv) wash your hands thoroughly after you have finished working on the brakes and certainly before you eat or smoke; v) replace shoes and pads only with asbestos-free shoes or pads. Note that asbestos brake dust can cause cancer if inhaled.

Brake fluid

• Brake fluid absorbs moisture rapidly from the air and can become dangerous resulting in brake failure. Castrol (U.K.) Ltd.

recommends that you should have your brake fluid tested at least once a year by a properly equipped garage and you should change the fluid in accordance with your vehicle manufacturer's recommendations or as advised in this book if we recommend a shorter interval than the manufacturer. You should buy no more brake fluid than you need, in smaller rather than larger containers. Never store an opened container of brake fluid. Dispose of the remainder at your Local Authority Waste Disposal Site, in the designated disposal unit, not with general waste or with waste oil.

Engine oils

• Take care to observe the following precautions when working with used engine oil. Apart from the obvious risk of scalding when draining the oil from a hot engine, there is the danger from contaminates that are contained in all used oil.

• Always wear disposable plastic or rubber gloves when draining the oil from your engine. Note that the drain plug and the oil are often hotter than you expect. Wear gloves if the plug is too hot to touch and keep your hand to one side so that you are not scalded by the spurt of oil as the plug comes away. There are very real health hazards associated with used engine oil. In the words of one manufacturer's handbook, "Prolonged and repeated contact may cause serious skin disorders, including dermatitis and cancer". Use a barrier cream on your hands and try not to get oil on them. Always wear gloves and wash your hands with hand cleaner soon after carrying out the work. Keep oil out of the reach of children.

Plastic materials

• Work with plastic materials brings additional hazards into workshops. Many of the materials used (polymers, resins, adhesives and materials acting as catalysts and accelerators), contain dangers in the form of poisonous fumes, skin irritants, and the risk of fire and explosions. Do not allow resin or 2-pack adhesive hardener, or that supplied with filler or 2-pack stopper, to come into contact with skin or eyes. Read carefully the safety notes supplied on the can, tube or packaging and always wear impervious gloves and goggles when working with them.

Fluoroelastomers

Most important! please read this section!
• If you service your vehicle in the normal

Safety 10. Keep your inspection lamp well away from any source of petrol (gasoline) such as when disconnecting a carburettor float bowl or fuel line.

OIL POLLUTES WATER USE YOUR BRAIN- NOT THE DRAIN!

Safety 11. When you drain your engine oil - don't oil the drain! Pouring oil down the drain will cause pollution. It is also an offence.

way, none of the following may be relevant to you. Unless, for example, you encounter a vehicle which has been on fire (even in a localised area), subject to heat in, say, a crash-damage repairer's workshop or a vehicle breaker's yard, or if any second-hand parts have been heated in any way.
• Many synthetic, rubber-like materials used in motor cars contain a substance called fluorine. These materials are known as fluoroelastomers and are commonly used for oil seals, wiring and cabling, bearing surfaces, gaskets, diaphragms, hoses and 'O' rings. If they are subjected to temperatures greater than 315 degrees C, they will decompose and can be potentially hazardous. Fluoroelastomer materials will show physical signs of decomposition under such conditions in the form of charring of black sticky masses. Some decomposition may occur at temperatures above 200 degrees C, and it is obvious that when a vehicle has been in a fire or has been dismantled with the assistance of a cutting torch or blow torch, the fluoroelastomers can decompose in the manner indicated above.
• In the presence of any water or humidity, including atmospheric moisture, the by-products caused by the fluoroelastomers being heated can be extremely dangerous. According to the Health and Safety Executive, "Skin contact with this liquid or decomposition residues can cause painful and penetrating burns. Permanent

irreversible skin and tissue damage can occur". Damage can also be caused to eyes or by the inhalation of fumes created as fluoroelastomers are burned or heated.

After a vehicle has been exposed to fire or high temperatures, you must observe the following precautions:

1. Do not touch blackened or charred seals or equipment.

2. Allow all burnt or decomposed fluoroelastomer materials to cool down before inspection, investigations, tear-down or removal.

3. Preferably, don't handle parts containing decomposed fluoroelastomers, but if you must, wear goggles and PVC (polyvinyl chloride) or neoprene protective gloves whilst doing so. Never handle such parts unless they are completely cool.

4. Contaminated parts, residues, materials and clothing, including protective clothing and gloves, should be disposed of by an approved contractor to landfill or by incineration according to national or local regulations. Oil seals, gaskets and 'O' rings, along with contaminated material, must not be burned.

PART III: GENERAL WORKSHOP SAFETY

• **Always** have a fire extinguisher of the

correct type at arm's length when working on the fuel system - under the vehicle, or under the bonnet. If you do have a fire, **don't panic**. Use the extinguisher effectively by directing it at the base of the fire.
• **Never** use a naked flame near petrol or anywhere in the workplace.
• **Never** use petrol (gasoline) to clean parts. Use paraffin (kerosene), white spirits, or best of all, a proprietary brand of degreaser.
• **No smoking**. There's a risk of fire or of transferring dangerous substances to your mouth and, in any case, ash falling into mechanical components is to be avoided.
• Be methodical in everything you do, use common sense, and think Safety First! at all times.

PART IV. ENVIRONMENT FIRST

• The used oil from the sump of just one car can cover an area of water the size of two football pitches, cutting off the oxygen supply and harming swans, ducks, fish and other river life.
• Don't mix used oil with other materials, such as paint and solvents, because this makes recycling difficult.
• Take used oil to an oil recycling bank. Telephone **free** in the UK on 0800 663366 to find the location of your nearest oil bank, or contact your local authority recycling officer.

Chapter 1
Buying a van for conversion

KNOW YOUR TRANSPORTERS

The original Transporter (split-windscreen or T1) was built from 1950 to 1967 and was replaced by the Bay Window model (or T2), from 1967 to 1980. Neither is covered here. The two models here are the last of the rear-engined Transporters, the T3 (1980-on), and the first of the front-engined vans, the T4, built from 1990 to 2003.

• Older versions, such as the T2 (South America) and T3 (South Africa) continued to be produced, sometimes in modified form, after the dates shown above.

• Water-cooled engines were fitted to the T3 from 1982.

• In 1991, VW called its new van the T4. Soon afterwards, it renamed the previous three models T1, T2 and T3. Very few people use the terms T1 and T2.

• The 2003-on van is the all-new T5.

• ALL VW vans are traditionally called 'Type 2', the Beetle being 'Type 1' and another VW saloon the 'Type 3'. Therefore, T3 vans are 'Type 2' NOT 'Type 3'.

• Other 'non-official' names for the 1980 to 1991 T3 include 'Type 25' (the digits '25' appear at the start of most T3 part numbers), 'Wedge' (which it emphatically isn't!), and others.

If you're buying a VW van for conversion, it's important that you buy right first time. It's too late after the vehicle's finished for you to decide that you don't like the base vehicle, so put some time into researching exactly what it is that you want from your motor caravan.

1-1. We're going to put the end at the start, so to speak, because that's what this book is all about - ending up with a motor caravan that you can use and enjoy. The author and his wife had this Volkswagen Transporter converted by Leisuredrive and, at the time of writing, the vehicle is still going strong. Here, it's parked at a Camping and Caravanning Club site at Hayfield in Derbyshire, a site only accessible to tent and motor caravan owners, not caravanners, because of the tight, tricky roads in the area - another advantage of VW Transporter motor caravanning!

• Does size matter? If so, you may be better off looking for a vehicle that's larger than the relatively compact Transporters.
• Is it important to squeeze every inch of space out of your van? Bear in mind that T3s have slightly more room inside than T4 models.

• Is a comfortable driving position, slick gearchange or automatic gearbox all-important? Then it's a T4 for you!
• Does speed matter? Do bear in mind that non-Turbo diesel VW vans are built with low power and high economy in mind and they can be relatively noisy. Van drivers are

expected to put up with the cacophony that comes from the front-engined T4 (T3s tend to leave the noise behind), and the low power that comes from non-Turbo diesel engines but you may find either or both of these just too irritating.
• Sophistication. If you test drive a van, do bear in mind that you will be driving it empty, whereas once the conversion has taken place, you will be driving it virtually fully laden the whole of the time, making it both quieter and more comfortable, though slower.
• The T3's Golf-based diesel engine is painfully under-powered and most drivers find them irritatingly slow. The T4's turbo-diesel is a real cracker, providing both performance and economy.

1-2. Our motor caravan is pictured here with another type of conversion from the same company, the Leisuredrive Crusader based on a later Volkswagen with front engine. This conversion has a fixed top as opposed to the raising top shown on our vehicle.

1-3. The van that we started off with was, in fact, a people carrier built by Volkswagen and called the Caravelle. If you start off with this type of vehicle, you won't have the time and expense of fitting side windows, though you will have to live with the window pattern created by the manufacturer, of course. You will also probably have better quality windows than those fitted to an aftermarket conversion. On the Volkswagen, the Caravelle's windows are recessed into the body panels, whereas converted windows have to be fitted to what were flat body panels and may, therefore, stick out a little further. In practice, though, you hardly notice the difference.

1-4. More typical is this commercial van, again a Volkswagen T3 with rear engine. This was an ideal vehicle for conversion because the bodywork was in superb condition and the mechanics had been well maintained, something that quite often - but not always! - happens with professionally maintained vehicles.

1-5. This was the interior of our Volkswagen Caravelle before work was started on it. The advantages of fold-down armrests were retained after the vehicle was converted, but the fully trimmed interior and rear seats were removed to make way for the conversion. In fact, we got a small amount by selling them which helped to offset some of the cost of conversion.

1-6. You may even be lucky and find the ideal van which has already been fitted with a high-top (if that's what you want).

1-7. Depending on how far you want to go, the condition of the front seats and the door trims will be worth noting. It's not unusual for owners to have the front seats retrimmed when a conversion is carried out, but if you can find a van with excellent trim, that's an extra expense saved.

Once you've decided which version of Transporter to go for you'll need to decide on the interior layout. Don't be surprised if, having gone through the process of deciding the layout you prefer, you revisit the type of van you want because the whole thing will be a balancing act between what you'd ideally like and what you can fit in. I mean, it's no good thinking you're going to be able to take the kitchen sink with you. (Oh then again, hang on a minute ...)

If you're going to 'scratch build' the interior, the only limits will be the dimensions of the van, the dimensions of the fixed components that you will be putting in, such as cooker and sink, and your own skills and imagination. On the other hand, you may choose to go for ready-made units and fit them to the van yourself. Leisuredrive, the company featured throughout this manual, manufactures such units for Volkswagen Transporters and you'll see them featured here. Again, if you're building your own from scratch, you still may be able to use the layouts designed by others as the basis for your units. Here are some typical features that you may wish to consider.

1-8. This Leisuredrive Crusader Volkswagen T4 layout is very typical of the most efficient use of space in a van of this size. The side sliding door gives good access to the 'living room' and the central area can still be used for carting things about when you're not on holiday.

1-9. Unlike the earlier Transporters with a rear engine, the underside of the rear seat and bed box are utilised for the portable WC and other storage space.

1-10. With a fixed high-top, there's certainly a greater feeling of airiness and there's also the potential for fitting 'upstairs' bunks for small children. Leisuredrive offers these as an optional extra.

1-11. When the rear seat area is turned into a bed, there's just enough room for getting up in the morning, putting the kettle on and getting dressed.

1-12. With the seat folded down, you can carry long loads from the DIY centre.

1-13. Of course, the T4 Transporter can also be fitted with an elevating roof.

1-14. Once again, the area beneath the seat box is invaluable as storage space for sleeping bags and the like.

1-15. Kitchen facilities in the raising roof models are exactly the same as those for fixed roof models. In all cases, you find you'll make far better use of the space if the front passenger seat is turned into a swivelling seat so that one of you can sit down without encroaching on the galley.

1-16. The Leisuredrive option is a low-line roof which gives you a good chance of being able to get under many car park barriers, depending on their height.

Visit Veloce on the web - www.veloce.co.uk

1-17. The wardrobe is generally lower in raising roof models. Some owners aspire to having a WC/shower compartment squeezed into this corner of the van on high-top models but, for obvious reasons, it's not possible on an elevating roof model.

1-21. This is the author's T3 Transporter with rear-mounted water-cooled engine on the day it came back home from Leisuredrive. The layout has proved to be a huge success in practice.
If you're wondering why it looks higher off the ground than others, it's because this is one of the 4WD Syncro models.

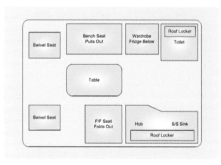

1-18. Whichever layout you choose, you will need to plan things out on a piece of paper. The best paper to use for your plans is squared paper so that you can get the proportions right, but the first step is to decide what will go where. This plan is only suitable for vans without a sliding side door where access is through the rear of the van.

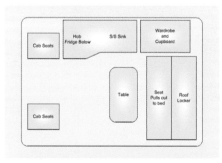

1-19. This type of layout is, of course, only suitable for vans with a sliding side door and, as you can see, there are then fewer options available with regard to where the kitchen facilities can be sited.

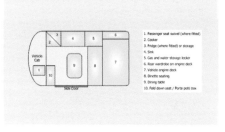

1-20. When you've got the rough layout in place, you'll need to make a plan like this one which is dimensionally and proportionally correct. You will also need to bear in mind the space to be taken up by whatever ancillaries you intend to install. For instance, a portable WC needs to be fitted neatly into a cupboard that isn't so large that it wastes space, while a water heater or space heater will have its own requirements, and you'll need to make sure that the cupboards and their shelves don't interfere with any such ancillaries.

1-22. Our Leisuredrive T3 Syncro has been seen at VW Type 2 Owners' Club events where there's an amazing amount of support for these vehicles, both from the many thousands of enthusiasts who attend the shows, and the parts specialists, such as JustKampers. The supply of parts from Volkswagen dealers is superb but you can often buy the parts more economically from the independent specialists. Find club and specialist names and addresses at the back of this book.

1-23. You'll want to preserve your VW Camper when it's finished. This is a professional type of injector for rust-prevention fluid and works from a compressor. Hand-pumped types are literally worse than useless. A part-coating of rust-prevention fluid concentrates rusting even more viciously on the unprotected areas.

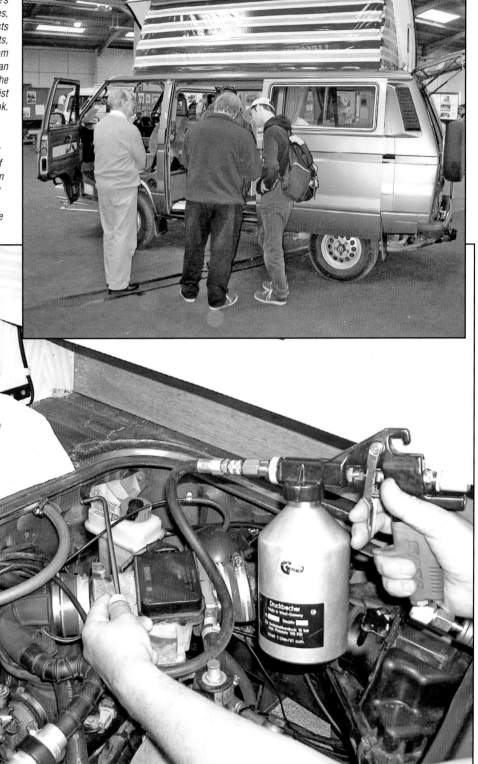

1-24. This JP Exhausts stainless steel exhaust on my Transporter is four years old. Only the clips and brackets are rusty.

1-25. If you choose this layout for your T4 Camper, you'll have the maximum amount of 'living room' space but a fairly minimal luggage bay and your rear visibility will be restricted too, which could be annoying when reversing.

1-26. Whichever layout you choose, remember that for most of the time you won't be using the vehicle on the camp site. Whichever route you go down, you'll have to make compromises. Just remember to make suitable allowances if your camper will also have to earn its keep as an everyday driver.

1-27. In 2003 the T5 Transporter appeared and, by 2004, there was already an Autokeepers camper conversion available.

Chapter 2
Exterior structural work

INTRODUCTION

There are several stages in converting the bodywork of a VW Transporter into a suitable shell for a motor caravan. In the case of the Volkswagen T3 Caravelle which we chose to have converted by Leisuredrive, there was less to do than would be required on a basic van - but there was still more than enough! In the case of the T4, there's a little more work involved.

First: You always start by stripping out the interior. On a T4 (front-engined) Volkswagen, there is more to do than on later vans. Later vans have more trim inside them, and usually more wiring to worry about. Caravelles have lots of interior, and you'll still need to take all the windows out so that the interior trim can be fitted later.

Most working vans have accumulated lots of 'muck' inside them so, once all the seats and trim are out of the way, you can pressure wash or steam clean the interior so that you're starting off with something that's completely clean - see Section 1.

Second: Any internal structural work - and indeed, any bodywork repairs that may be needed - can best be carried out now. Welding is most safely carried out without flammable trim in the area, but do remember to cover up any exposed glass, including dashboard and mirrors,

---

Top tips!
1. Some T4 vans have a bulkhead panel running right across the van, behind the cab seats, and this has to be removed.
2. Removing the seats: on some T4 models there are four vertical bolts, but on others there are two bolts at the back and two clips at the front. You take out the two bolts from the back and then tip the seat forward slightly and pull back, disconnecting the seat from its clips.

---

before using an angle grinder. The sparks etch themselves into any nearby glass or paintwork.

Third: Now it's on to some of the most dramatic parts of the conversion job. This stage involves making fundamental changes to the vehicle's bodywork so that it can fulfil its new purpose and is described in the rest of this Chapter.

Before starting work, you'll need to decide what type of roof you want to have. All have pros and cons, so it's a matter of seeing which one is likely to suit you best.

HIGH-TOP OR ELEVATING ROOF?
High-top
• You've always got lots of headroom,

making moving around easier.
• You won't be able to get into any car parks with height barriers.
• You won't have to go outside to raise the roof when it's raining.
• The wind will blow you around more as you drive and your top speed will be lower and fuel economy worse.
• Bear in mind that some high-tops are higher than others. Some have room for (cramped) kids' beds 'upstairs' while others are just high enough to stand up in.

Elevating roof
• You'll park more easily and the speed, stability and economy will hardly be affected.
• It gets colder inside at night with the top up, because you have, in effect, a tent over you. (It's warmer if you close the top at night, if there are two of you).
• You can park in some car parks with height restrictions, though by no means all of them.
• There may be a little more maintenance needed, long-term, as struts wear or if the fabric becomes damaged.

SELF-BUILD OR NOT SELF-BUILD?
Some owners like to have the work of fitting a high- or lifting-top (and often, the fitting of side windows), carried out for

them. Companies such as Leisuredrive cater for all requirements, giving you the choice between having:

• All the work carried out for you. You deliver the bare van then later, you collect the finished motor caravan. Time: A week or so.

• The hardtop or elevating roof and windows fitted for you. You buy the internal furniture and kitchen equipment in kit form and fit them yourself. Time: A day or two for fitting; several weeks of solid work to fit out the interior, the details such as trimming taking longest.

• You buy all of the parts: roof, windows, trim and interior, and fit the lot yourself. Time: Several months of part-time work, if you've never done it before.

SECTION 1. PREPARING THE BARE VAN

The first job is always to clean out the inside of the van, unless it's a brand new one, of course.

The other point to consider is whether the bodywork will need attention before the conversion is carried out. In the case of our VW Caravelle, the surface rust scabs which disfigured the body were first dealt with and the bodywork was resprayed. However, there's an argument for respraying the vehicle after the conversion has been carried out because of the risk of paintwork damage during the conversion process. On the other hand, there will be less preparation needed, less to mask off and less risk of getting overspray onto your new interior if the respray is carried out first.

Any internal structural work can best be carried out now. Welding is most safely carried out without flammable trim in the area, but do remember to cover up any exposed glass, including dashboard and mirrors, before using an angle grinder. The sparks etch themselves immovably into any nearby glass or paintwork.

Some VW T4 vans have a bulkhead panel running right across the van, behind the cab seats and this has to be removed - see Chapter 3.

SECTION 2. FITTING SIDE WINDOWS

In all cases (except the most Spartan of conversions - not the sort covered here), the van will be fitted with windows. You really do need a bit of experience - or be prepared to take a lot of care - before carrying out this work yourself. You'll also need to invest in a few tools. The biggest difficulty will be for those whose vans have a lot of internal strengthening ribs

2-1-1. You always start by stripping out the interior. On a T4 (front-engined) Volkswagen, there is more to do than on earlier VW vans. Later vans have more trim inside them, and usually more wiring to worry about. People-carrier versions, such as the Caravelle, have lots of interior fittings to remove, and you'll still need to take all the windows out so that the new interior trim can be fitted later.

at the points where the windows have to be fitted. These have to be cut carefully away, leaving strength and neatness in the surrounding panels. Then it's a matter of marking the positions of the windows onto the side panels, allowing 3 or 4 mm extra, over the size of the sheet of glass, to allow for the thickness of the rubbers. Start with a drill, then transfer to a jigsaw with a blade

suitable for thin steel and cut the panel out. It's essential that the bare edges are cleaned up and painted, and the glass fitted correctly so as to avoid leaks - a job for your local car windscreen fitting company perhaps? Here's how Leisuredrive carries out the job of fitting side windows to T3 and T4 models.

2-1-2. Most working vans have accumulated lots of 'muck' inside them and so, once all the seats and trim are out of the way, you can pressure wash or steam clean the interior so that you're starting off with something that's completely clean.

2-2-1. This T3 Transporter van has already had its new high-top roof fitted and is now ready for the side windows to be fitted.

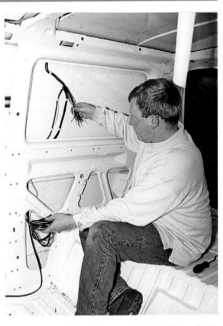

2-2-2. Barry Plumridge starts by identifying all of the wiring so that it can be safely removed. Where it's connected to components, such as a rear interior light, the connections should be removed and it may even be necessary to cut the wiring in some places in order to remove it safely and re-route it where necessary.

2-2-3. Barry uses an air chisel to cut through both ends of this strengthening rail and also to cut between the rail and the outer panel where the two are bonded together with strong sealant. Hand tools would work just as well; they'd just be slower.

2-2-4. Barry now removes the rail exposing the panel to be cut away.

2-2-5. On T4 models, the sliding door interior handle is adjacent to where the glass will be fitted and the handle must be removed first.

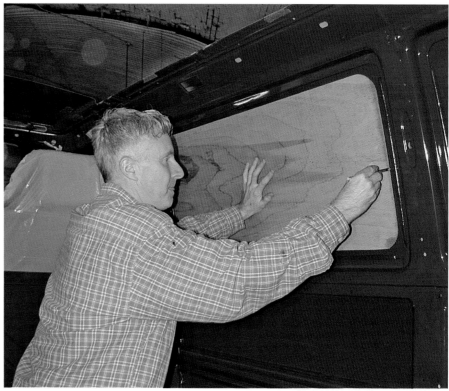

2-2-6. Leisuredrive's works manager Barry Roberts (we'll call him Barry R), demonstrates how to use a template to mark the position of the holes to be drilled for cutting out the window. The template is being held up to the inside of the van and four marks made, one on each side of the template. If you do this yourself, it's best to use a card template and tape it to the panel, or have an assistant hold it, making absolutely certain that it doesn't move at all.

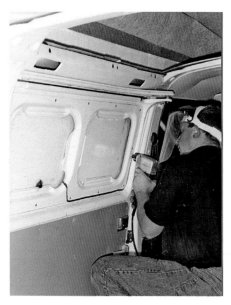

2-2-7. Back on the T3, Barry Plumridge cuts out the internal strengthening panels on the inside of the sliding door before starting on the outer panel.

2-2-8. Barry R drills a hole from the inside of the caravan at each of the marks he has made ...

2-2-9. ... creating four small holes in all.

2-2-10. Barry R now takes a pair of pencils and tapes them together like this.

2-2-11. He now uses the company's well-used template to mark out the position of the side window. You would have to make up your own from plywood using the glass as a guide. The small hole he drilled earlier is used as a lining-up point to establish the correct position of the board.

2-2-12. It's best to use a felt pen to mark the position of the board so that you will notice if it slips. Barry now uses the two pencils shown earlier to draw a line all the way around the board. The idea of the two pencils is that they are held perpendicular to the line of the board so that the outer pencil gives you a cutting line, which is very slightly larger than the board itself. This is necessary because after the steelwork has been cut out, the rubber that holds the glass in place will have a thickness and it's to allow for this that the extra cutting width is marked.

2-2-13. Before beginning to use the jigsaw, Barry R uses the drill once more to make an elongated hole, large enough to insert the jigsaw blade.

2-2-14. Before using a jigsaw to cut out the unwanted steel, Barry R covers the shoe of the jigsaw with fresh masking tape so that it doesn't mark the paintwork.

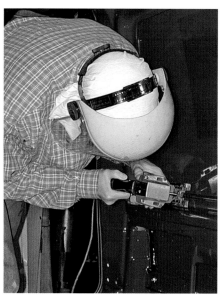

2-2-15. In this instance, Barry R is cutting out the panel from the inside because, in this case, the cut is adjacent to the strengthening rib, so no marking out was necessary.

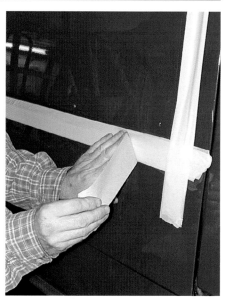

2-2-16. Where the cut has to be made from the outside, Barry puts several strips of wide masking tape over the paintwork that he doesn't want to be damaged.

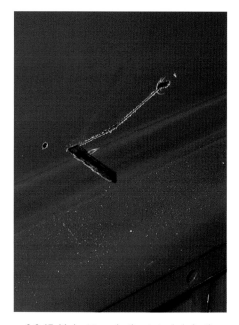

2-2-17. It's best to make the starter hole for the jigsaw a little way inboard of the cutting line, then redirect the cutting position of the jigsaw precisely to the line, obviating the risk of the starter hole having been drilled in the wrong place.

2-2-18. Wearing the obligatory eye protection, Barry cuts carefully to the outer of the two pencil lines.

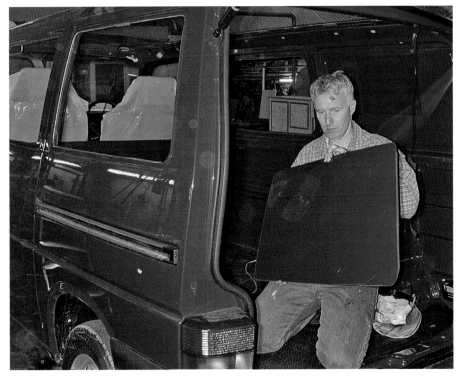

2-2-19. As the last part of the cut is made, you will need to have someone else inside the van supporting the panel as it comes free.

SAFETY FIRST!

• You must always wear eye protection when working with power tools.
• You must also wear heavy-duty industrial gloves when handling cut steelwork. Barry R refuses to do so but you will notice that Barry P always wears safety gloves (as does the author of this book), and it is essential that you should do so.

2-2-21. If you're going to err, make sure that the error is on the inside of the panel being cut out and not the outside because it's virtually impossible to put metal back in again! Barry goes around trimming his cuts to the exact position of his pencil line.

FITTING THE GLASS

The following pictures and captions will guide you through the steps involved in this procedure.

2-2-22. Most glass held in with rubbers has a spreader strip fitted to the rubber after the glass and rubber have been fitted to the vehicle to hold the glass in firmly. This is chromed plastic spreader strip and looks particularly attractive on a motor caravan conversion.

2-2-20. Barry removes the now redundant panel from the van - still not wearing gloves, as he should!

2-2-23. Most people use nylon string for this but Barry R chooses to use electrical cable. There is a lip in the rubber which fits over the steel bodywork and, to start off with, the cord (or cable) has to be pushed into this lip all the way around the rubber and then continued so that the ends of the cord overlap by about 150mm (6in). The rubber has, of course, already been fitted to the glass on the workbench.

2-2-24. This is most important! Barry uses silicone spray all the way around the outer edge of the rubber to help it to slip over the steel panel. You could, alternatively, use washing-up liquid diluted with a little water.

2-2-25. Barry R offers up the glass and rubber, places it first in position at the bottom of the panel and then pushes firmly at the top.

2-2-26. This different fitting sees Barry R on the inside of the vehicle pulling on the cord that he'd previously fitted to the rubber so that the rubber lip is eased over the panel. Note the two ghostly faces on the outside of the vehicle!

2-2-27. They're there for a very important reason: the glass has to be pushed firmly inwards as the rubber lip is pulled over the panel on the inside.

2-2-28. Barry P fits this sliding glass panel, which is done in a completely different way, the surround being fitted to the bodywork first.

2-2-29. The sliding panel is then slotted in from above ...

2-2-30. ... pushed into position, and the lip on the previously-fitted outer panel is eased over the sliding glass frame.

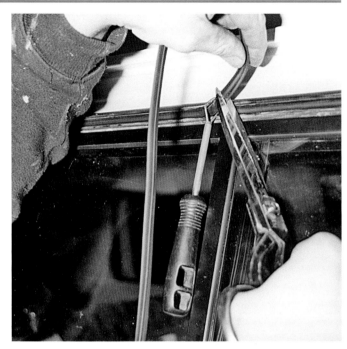

2-2-32. Note the special tool which is virtually essential if you are to have any hope of getting the rubber into place. You will also need lots of lubricant, such as the silicone spray or washing-up liquid described earlier. When all of the filler strip is in position, the insertion tool is left in place and the strip is cut off with scissors, slightly too long so that it has to be pushed back in on itself. Over the years to come, it will shrink anyway. Make sure that the joint is at the top to reduce any risk of water ingress.

2-2-31. Now the spreader strip that was shown earlier on a different type of glass fitting is pushed into place in the slot in the retaining rubber.

2-2-33. Barry P admires the finished sliding glass fitted in the cooking area of this conversion.

2-2-34. This time Barry R is fitting a VW Original-Equipment bonded glass. He starts by attaching the rubber to the glass as with other types.

2-2-35. After working the rubber all the way around the glass, Barry R carefully establishes the point at which the two ends of the rubber overlap.

2-2-36. He uses a sharp knife blade to cut both ends of the rubber so that they are completely flat and square at the point where they will face each other.

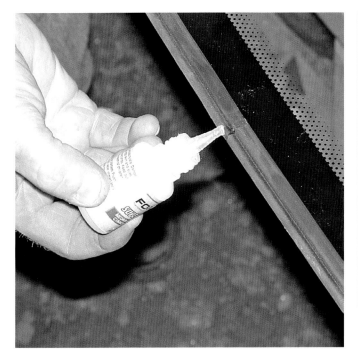

2-2-37. The ends of the rubber need to be bonded together with special rubber adhesive.

2-2-38. The adhesive for holding the glass and rubber in the panel work has to be used in conjunction with these special primers. After cleaning all traces of contaminants from the metalwork, glass and rubber, one type of primer is used on the van body while the other is used on the glass. The one for the glass obviously has to be applied before the rubber is fitted to the glass.

2-2-39. Barry starts by applying sealant to the rubber where it will be held against the vehicle's bodywork.

2-2-40. After making the joint scrupulously clean with the proprietary cleaner that comes with the kit, he applies activator to the area of the joint.

2-2-41. Barry now offers up and fits the new glass into position on the vehicle, holding it in place while the rapid bonding takes effect.

2-2-42. Barry also demonstrates a bonded-in sliding-glass window frame, which looks a little neater than the type fitted by Barry P to the T3 Transporter because the frame is narrower.

SECTION 3. MAKING AND PREPARING A HIGH-TOP

The following pictures and captions will guide you through the steps involved in this procedure.

2-3-1. Leisuredrive makes all of its own fibreglass panels. This is a new high-top roof being laid-up (as the fibreglassing term is), in the appropriate mould.

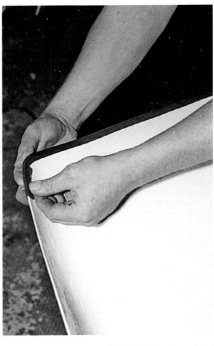

2-3-3. The raw edges are finished with trim material - rubber edging strip.

2-3-2. The wooden reinforcements have now been added and the top is lifted out of the mould after the edges have been trimmed off.

2-3-4. This is a different top but the principle remains the same. The position of the side window is being marked out with a template ...

2-3-5. ... before being cut out with a jigsaw.

2-3-6. The inside of this top is now prepared for fitting the interior trim by coating it with adhesive.

SAFETY FIRST!
• It is essential to always wear an efficient particle mask or air-fed breathing mask when machining fibreglass because the particles are potentially extremely injurious to health.

2-3-8. ... and carefully rolled flat to promote good adhesion and provide a smooth finish.

2-3-7. The new trim material is lowered into place ...

2-3-9. Now it's time to fit the side trim boards.

2-3-10. Window apertures are cut through the side trim boards and then the insides of the hard top can be finished off with trim material.

2-3-11. The rubber is cut to length so that the ends provide a tight fit. The ends are the glued together with superglue.

2-3-12. Glazing rubber is added to the edge of the window aperture.

2-3-13. With the aid of silicone lubricant, the glass is inserted into the base of the rubber ...

2-3-14. ... and eased into the slot in the rubber all the way round.

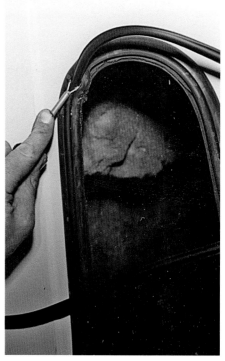

2-3-15. Spreader strip is inserted into the groove in the outer edge of the rubber to spread it and hold the glass tightly in place. It's almost impossible to do this without the correct insertion tool shown here.

2-3-16. The spreader strip is cut to length and the ends butted carefully together. The high-top is now ready for fitting to the vehicle.

SECTION 4. FITTING A HIGH-TOP TO T3 TRANSPORTERS
The following pictures and captions will guide you through the steps involved in this procedure.

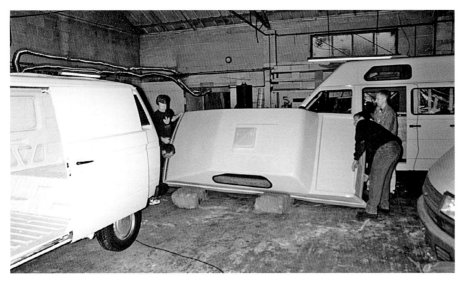

2-4-1. The lads at Leisuredrive get ready to fit a Lo-Line high-top roof, designed to be high enough so that you can stand up in the back of the van. Alternatively, there's the (predictably named) Hi-Line roof, as seen on the van in the background, which is intended to provide the option of 'upstairs' sleeping space for small children.

2-4-3. It's now essential to make sure that the top is seated precisely in the correct position before moving on. Head scratching is optional ...

2-4-2. The roof has been cut out in similar style to that shown for the van photographed for the next section. Note that no extra bracings are needed on the T3 Transporter for this particular roof but it is essential that you check with Leisuredrive or your high-top supplier if fitting other tops, or when working on other models of van. In some cases, extra strengthening braces will be necessary.
As you can see, with some of the chaps standing on the outside and others on the inside of the van, it's just possible to lift the top into place. Note that the rubber sealing strip has already been fitted to the front of the high-top.

2-4-4. Leisuredrive's Barry starts to bond the roof into place on the van. This is another larger van with a Hi-Top roof being fitted but the principle is exactly the same. Barry starts by applying masking tape all the way around the lower edge of the roof so that excess sealer is easier to get off. Once again, you should check with your roof supplier on the type of sealer that is recommended for this particular work. My own preference would be to use a Wurth sealer and you can ask your Wurth supplier for data sheets which will advise on the correct sealer to use with GRP and steel, and also on the correct way of using it. In general, it's essential that all the surfaces to be bonded are thoroughly cleaned with panel wipe so that no trace of dirt or grease - even invisible grease from your fingers - can remain on either of the surfaces to be bonded together.

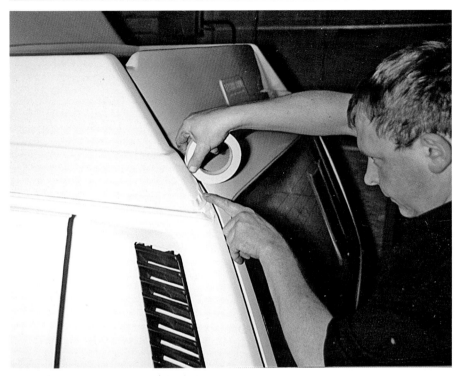

2-4-5. Barry takes his time with the masking tape, especially around the tricky shapes where the doors are fitted.

2-4-6. If you are retaining the colour of the vehicle's bodywork and also that of the high-top, it's a good idea to try to use a sealer which is the same colour as the bodywork.

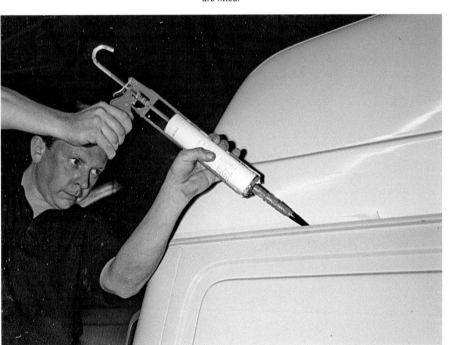

2-4-7. In this case, the whole of the van will be resprayed, so Barry uses regular black sealer. It's most important to achieve a consistent run of sealer with no gaps and with lots of sealer in place to not only prevent the ingress of water, but also to add to the strength of the two panels being bonded together.

2-4-8. From the point of view of strength, sealer applied to the inside, where it can be injected between the van's bodywork and the high-top, is even more important. Once again, make absolutely certain that there are no gaps and that there is sufficient sealer to bond the top in place.

Top tip!
Just in case you won't be able to get sealer down between the two panels once the top is in place, be sure to apply a large quantity of bonding sealer to the roof of the van at the point where the high-top will sit on it.

2-4-9. Barry finishes off the outside by peeling off the masking tape and then wiping down the bodywork where excess sealer may have oozed out. In his case, there was no wiping down to do because Barry has done this job many times before!

2-4-10. If you intend fitting a luggage rack to the rear of this type of high-top, note that Leisuredrive bonds timbers into the structure so that the luggage rack can be screwed down. Be sure to use sealer beneath each of the feet and in each of the screw holes so that there is no possibility of water getting in.

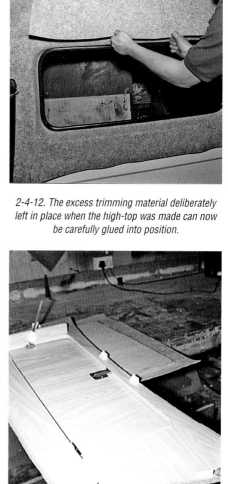

2-4-12. The excess trimming material deliberately left in place when the high-top was made can now be carefully glued into position.

2-4-13. The Leisuredrive roof furniture, which comes ready-made, has brackets fitted to it.

2-4-11. There's a recess at the top of the van sides, where the hard top is fitted, which is impossible to trim successfully. Leisuredrive screws a panel to the top of the van side-wall (into a hollow box-section, of course), so the screws won't show through on the outside!

2-4-14. These brackets enable you to offer up the furniture and screw it into place in the correct, pre-determined position. Note that the wiring has been run into this particular model's construction ready for fitting an interior light.

2-4-15. Back on the Volkswagen T3, Barry is fitting the shallow cupboard at the rear of the van's steel roof.

2-4-16. There are no brackets in this case, so Barry drills through the strut on the cupboard and into the rib which runs across the roof.

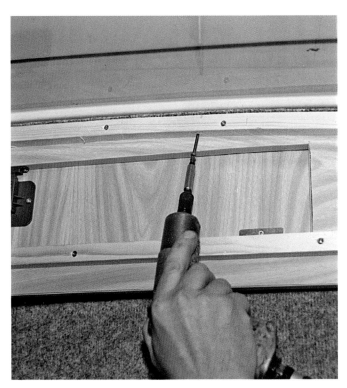

2-4-17. An appropriate size and length of self-tapping screw is driven into the rib. It's important that the screw isn't too long, or it will push right through the rib and damage the roof.

2-4-18. At the rear of what will become the shallow cupboard, another timber panel is screwed to the van's bodywork. It then only remains to screw the cupboard base onto these two panels to form an enclosed, shallow storage cupboard.

SECTION 5. FITTING A HIGH-TOP TO A T4 TRANSPORTER

In some respects - particularly to do with reinforcing and strengthening - fitting a high-top to the T4 Transporter follows the approach described for the T4 elevating roof in Section 7, so it may be useful to refer to that section too.

The process of fitting a high-top to a T4 Transporter is similar to that of a T3 only in the sense that you have to cut a hole in the van roof before you can fit the new high-top. In other respects, there are significant differences. Leisuredrive has developed a strengthening framework which needs to go around the perimeter of the cut-out roof to give it back its missing strength. I photographed different vehicles being converted and the photographs in this section are an amalgamation of those vehicles.

2-5-1. Barry P starts by drilling a hole in the roof to give him a datum point from which to carry out his measurements.

2-5-2. Barry now moves to the outside of the roof and, using the drilled hole positions as his starting point, marks out the precise cut lines for removing the old roof.

2-5-3. The cut lines follow the swages in the roof panel. Barry cuts along the roof with a jigsaw.

2-5-4. He has also drilled a hole in each corner to enable the jigsaw to easily go round the bend.

2-5-5. In the foreground of this shot you can just see that strips of timber have been placed beneath the corners of the roof as it's being cut away to stop it from dropping into the space beneath. With one person standing inside the van, two more help to lift the redundant roof panel away from the vehicle.

2-5-6. The panel is fairly heavy and is also dangerous because of the sharpness of the cut edges.

SAFETY FIRST!
• Unlike the guys in this and the previous shot, you are strongly recommended to wear heavy-duty industrial gloves whenever handling or working with cut sheet materials.

2-5-7. If there are any jagged edges around the roof, or swarf left from the jigsaw blade, now is the time for a clean up. The edges are now painted with metal primer and then with finish coat to protect them against corrosion.

2-5-8. This is Barry R on another conversion, offering up the rear strengthening rib which goes across the rear end of the roof.

2-5-9. Barry P applies adhesive to the rib and clamps it in place.

2-5-10. The roof panel can then be drilled and the strengthening rib riveted into place at each end.

2-5-12. Barry P has applied adhesive to the top of this front strengthening panel and is being assisted in offering it up to its correct position beneath the roof.

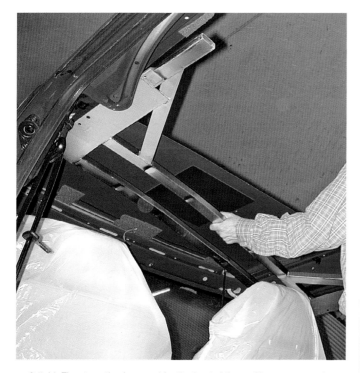

2-5-11. The strengthening panel for the front of the roof is a more complex affair, and is shown here being offered up next. It has to be carefully located, and you will notice that the front end of the roof has not been entirely cut away to fit the shape of the strengthening panel, for reasons which will become obvious later. Barry R is going to temporarily fit the strengthener and drill the necessary holes in the roof before removing it and moving on to the next stage.

2-5-13. Seen from beneath, the strengthener is now riveted permanently into place on the underside of the roof.

2-5-14. These side panels have a function which is both decorative and structural.

2-5-15. Barry R offers the new side panel up to the side of the roof and checks it for fit.

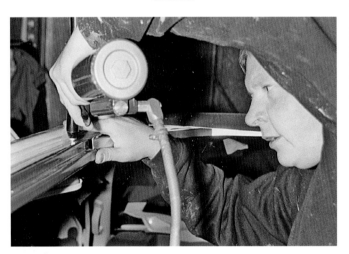

2-5-16. When the fit has been confirmed, it can be bonded and riveted into place.

2-5-17. More rivet holes have to be drilled to attach the side panel to the hollow strengthening section at the side of the roof, and note that if any wiring needs to be put in position, such as that for an interior light, you may need to drill a hole and pass the cable through in the appropriate position (arrowed).

2-5-18. Barry R rivets the panel in place.

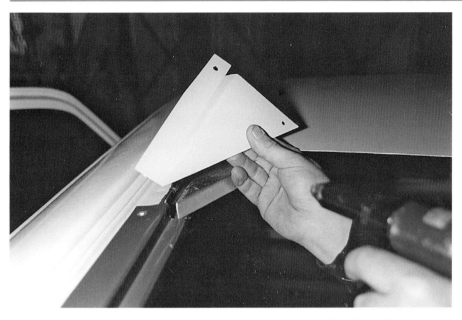

2-5-19. Up top side again, Barry P demonstrates the plate that connects the side rail to the front reinforcing section.

2-5-20. Barry applies adhesive, holds the plate in place with a clamp, drills where necessary and rivets it in place. Note the way in which Barry fits a rivet into each hole as he drills it to make sure that all the holes remain lined up.

2-5-21. Here you can see all the rivets have been fitted between roof and front reinforcing panel and now the remaining superfluous material in the roof can be cut away to match the shape and size of the reinforcer ...

2-5-22... leaving the interior view looking like this, identical with the reinforcer used for elevating roof models.

2-5-23. As a final step, the reinforcer is bolted to the roof panel where necessary.

2-5-24. The finished roof aperture now looks impressively large and it's this that provides a good deal of usable space on the inside of the Leisuredrive T4 conversion - more open space than you can achieve on the inside of a T3.

2-5-25. As with the T3 roof, the new high-top will be bonded down to the van roof. It's absolutely essential that every trace of both dirt and any other contaminant, such as silicone, is removed from the roof. Barry P wipes all of the area to be bonded with proprietary panel wipe, obtained from any Autopaint factor (or see Autopaint's address in the index of this book).

2-5-26. This is one type of Leisuredrive's high-top roofs being lifted into position. Hope none of them are ticklish!

2-5-27. And this is another type of roof. The procedure is exactly the same for each and at least one person has to be on the inside of the van to help lift the roof in place. Before being lifted off the ground, sealant has been applied to the edge of the roof all the way around at the point where it touches the edge of the van roof.

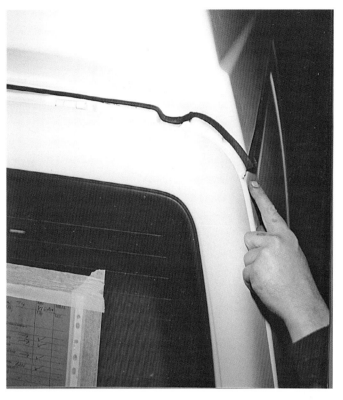

2-5-28. It's now essential to check that the position of the high-top is exactly correct and that the edging strip remains in place on the fibreglass panel.

2-5-29. More adhesive needs to be 'gunned' into place from the inside of the van to make sure that there is an adequate quantity between the two panels to be bonded together.

2-5-30. The bonding agent sets firmly, and it's essential to go all the way around the van wiping off the excess where it oozes out.

2-5-31. Wiping off excess sealant is something that the Leisuredrive fitters do very thoroughly. It's extremely difficult to get every last trace off unless you go around the van several times. With the high-top fitted and finished, you've now got the basis of a motor caravan conversion to start working on.

2-5-32. A converted Leisuredrive motorhome, complete with newly fitted high-top roof.

SECTION 6. FITTING AN ELEVATING ROOF TO A T3 TRANSPORTER

An elevating roof on a T3 Transporter involves cutting a smaller opening in the roof than on later vehicles. It can provide you with extra room for standing up in the living area and presents lots of access for storage space over the cab and the seat and engine areas. This sequence follows the fitting procedure as carried out on our own 1985 Caravelle Syncro.

The steel frame supplied by Leisuredrive sets the dimensions to be used for cutting out. The exact location of the aperture will be governed, says Leisuredrive, by the position of the front and centre stays of the elevating roof - see illustration 6-14. Leisuredrive should be able to supply an exact measurement of its recommended position of the aperture though it seems that its exact location is not critical. Alternatively, note the position of the aperture relative to the pressed swages in the roof seen in the photographs in this section.

SAFETY FIRST!
• You must always wear adequate eye protection when working with power tools.
• When working with the cut edges of metal, you must always wear heavy-duty industrial gloves even though Barry chooses not to do so throughout this sequence.

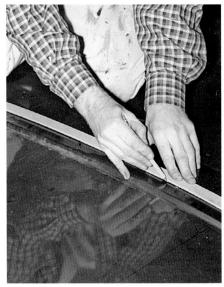

2-6-1. Leisuredrive's foreman, Barry Roberts, starts by marking out the correct cut lines on the top of the roof.

2-6-2. Jigsaws are happier cutting straight lines than going round tight curves, so Barry drills a hole in each corner large enough for the jigsaw blade to enter.

2-6-3. The early part of the cut is straightforward because there is still plenty of strength in the roof.

2-6-4. As the cut continues, the part of the roof being cut away begins to sag. Barry cuts front-to-back along each side of the vehicle ...

2-6-5. ... then cuts across the back and from back-to-front down each side of the vehicle. Note that the loose end of the panel has been supported with a strip of wood to prevent it from folding down.

2-6-6. Now, as he lifts the redundant panel away, Barry has pulled on his heavy-duty gloves.

2-6-7. Whenever cutting out with a jigsaw, there is inevitably a little roughness left along the cut. The steel is thin so it's too risky to clean it up with an angle grinder. Barry uses a file.

2-6-8. All traces of swarf can now be removed.

2-6-9. All bare edges are now treated with metal primer.

SAFETY FIRST!
• You should always wear adequate eye protection whenever blowing debris with an airline.

2-6-10. The pre-formed Leisuredrive strengthening frame is now lowered into position on the vehicle.

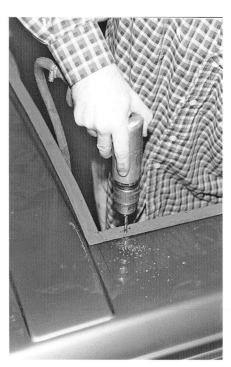

2-6-11. Barry uses the pre-drilled holes in the frame to drill through the roof panel ...

2-6-12. ... then coats the head of each rivet with more paint to protect the drilled hole ...

2-6-13. ... and rivets the framework into place.

2-6-14. Now it's time to fit the mounting points for the elevating roof struts. The exact positions are supplied with the kit and Barry makes sure that the position is correct before using a felt pen to mark around the mounting plate so that its correct position can be maintained.

2-6-15. This is the front strut mounting being fitted to the roof by first drilling through the pre-drilled holes in the mounting plate.

2-6-16. After drilling, the mounting plates are both riveted down as with the roof cut-out reinforcing frame.

2-6-17. At this stage, the structural work has been carried out on the roof and Barry starts to position the elevating roof hinges, which are fitted on the opposite side to the sliding door.

2-6-18. The position of each hinge is carefully measured and marked on the roof.

2-6-19. As well as being fitted to the curved section of the roof, each hinge is also riveted to the drip rail.

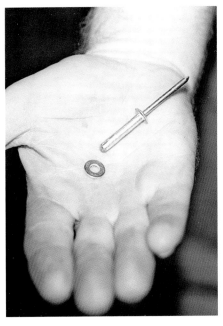

2-6-20. Each hinge puts a lot of pressure on a relatively small area, and it's important to use a washer on the inside of the roof panel on each rivet to help spread the load.

2-6-21. Barry rivets the hinge to the drip channel ...

2-6-22. ... and then to the roof proper.

2-6-23. The elevating roof has been removed from the mould and Barry starts to prepare it for use on the vehicle.

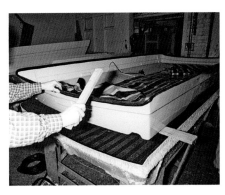

2-6-24. The seal and edge finishing strip is tapped fully home all the way around.

2-6-25. The joint in the seal is made at the rear where there is less risk of water ingress.

2-6-26. It takes four people to manoeuvre the elevating roof out of the fibreglassing bay.

2-6-28. With three people lifting the roof on the outside, one stands inside and helps to manoeuvre it into place through the opening in the van roof.

2-6-27. You need plenty of room to lift the roof up and onto the top of the vehicle. Start with the roof on its edge on the sliding-door side with the folding fabric hanging down like a curtain.

2-6-29. Front-to-rear and side-to-side, the elevating top is carefully positioned on the roof of the vehicle.

2-6-30. Barry takes care to lever the seal down behind the hinge so that the former doesn't foul on the latter.

2-6-31. The new seal needs to be under compression when the hinges are fitted, and the best way of ensuring that this is the case is to have someone sit on the corner of the roof while the hinge positions are drilled and the rivets fitted.

2-6-32. Once again, at the rear of the vehicle and with someone putting their weight on the top of the roof, Barry drills the positions for the rear hinges ...

2-6-33. ... and rivets the hinge into place while the weight is still on the roof, holding it in position. Note that the washers shown earlier must also be used on the insides of fibreglass when it is being riveted because if you try to rivet onto raw fibreglass, the rivet head can easily pull through.

2-6-34. From inside the vehicle the elevating roof can now be pushed upwards.

2-6-35. It's essential that the roof is held open by the correct amount: Leisuredrive uses a pair of pre-cut wooden batons to ensure that the elevating roof opening is correct. The correct length of each baton is 47 inches.

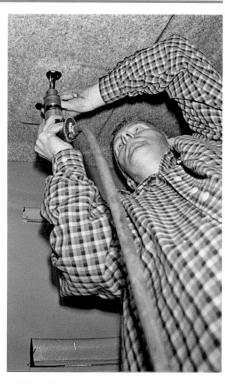

2-6-36. Barry now screws the pull handle to the wooden plate that has been built into the fibreglass roof. He'll need this later on because otherwise there'll be no means of pulling the roof down again.

2-6-37. The tubular framework for the elevating roof section may need the holes in the ends of the frame drilling out in order to take the pivot bolts.

2-6-38. The frame ends are connected to the pivots with the bolts and nuts supplied.

2-6-39. Threadlock is used on each bolt to ensure that the nuts can't come unscrewed. It isn't possible to tighten the nuts because, of course, the frames need to be able to pivot freely.

2-6-40. The elevating roof frames are slotted into place through the pockets sewn to the elevating roof fabric.

2-6-42. The correct positions of the pivots on the van roof can now be established. The fabric ends must be vertical and all of the tubular socket connections correctly made. The pivots can now be drilled and riveted down to the van roof.

2-6-43. Each end of the roof has a pair of struts to help the roof to be raised easily and smoothly, to hold it when it's up and allow it to come down again smoothly. The struts and their pivots come as a kit of components which need to be assembled.

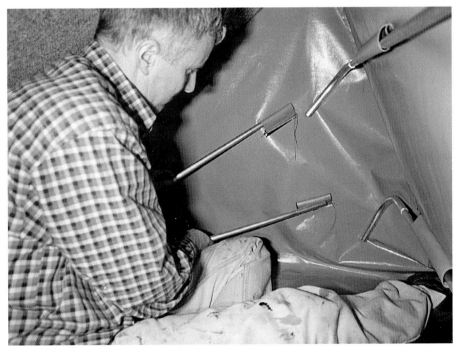

2-6-41. Similarly, the pivot arms are slotted through the pockets on the ends of the fabric and push-fitted into the longitudinal arms.

2-6-44. Each strut fits to its plastic pivot with a pivot pin and spring clip.

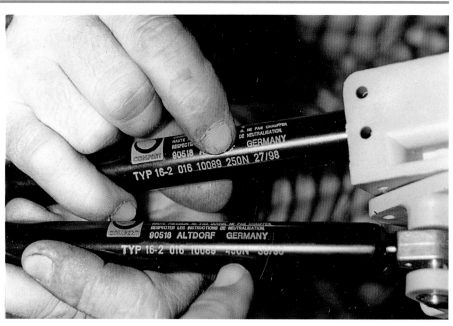

2-6-45. With the pivot pin in place, the spring clip pushes into a groove in the end of the pivot pin, preventing it from coming out again.

*2-6-46. It's important to note that the two struts for each end each have a different rating. There are two struts rated 250N and two rated 450N. **It is most important that the more upright of the two struts has the 450N rating while the more angled of the two struts has the 250N rating.***

2-6-47. Barry starts off by fitting the more upright of the two struts. The bottom of the strut locates in a hole in the mounting plate that's already been fitted to the roof. The position of the top of the strut is established when the strut is fully expanded, and the bottom mounting is in place, at which point the strut should be more or less vertical.

2-6-48. The strut pivot mounting position is drilled with a suitably small drill to allow the screw to bite into the wooden backing inside the fibreglass elevating roof.

Top tips!
• If you fit the upright strut incorrectly the strut will close before the roof comes down.
• If this is the case it should be adjusted accordingly.

2-6-49. The pivot is now held to the roof with suitable screws.

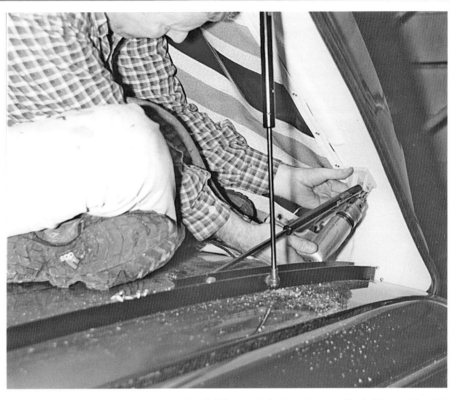

2-6-50. For the angle strut, the same procedure is followed: the bottom strut mounting is fitted and the strut fully expanded. This establishes the position for the pivot which is drilled and screwed to the elevating roof.

2-6-51. The elevating roof fabric is now sealed to the van roof. A plastic strip holds the fabric down to the steelwork. Holes are drilled through the strip into the steel ...

2-6-52. ... and self-tapping screws used to hold the sealing strip down. Alternatively, of course, pop rivets could be used.

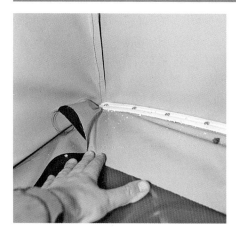

2-6-53. Once the fabric has been held down all the way around, surplus can be cut off with a craft knife.

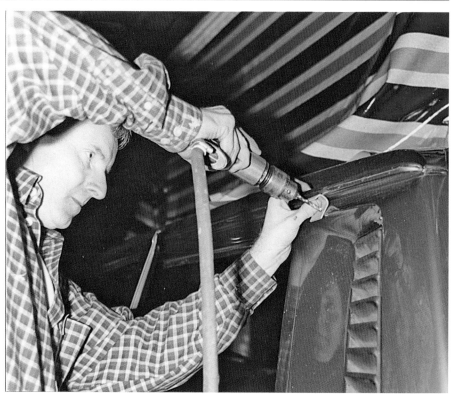

2-6-55. At the rear, the clip is fitted just behind the rear-most window. Barry is pre-drilling the holes ...

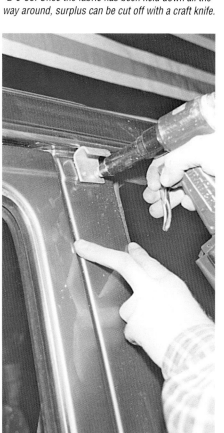

2-6-54. Back on the outside of the van and Barry starts to fit the clips for holding the roof down when it is lowered. The front-most clip is fitted to the vehicle B-pillar, drilled and riveted centrally on the pillar and pushed up against the underside of the drip rail.

2-6-56. ... before riveting the corrosion-resistant, plated clip onto the body.

2-6-57. The over-centre catch which pulls down onto this clip must be fitted precisely centrally over the clip.

2-6-58. Barry marks the position of each fixing hole precisely with a pencil.

2-6-59. If he now just drilled through the fibreglass, he would also drill through the elevating roof fabric! To prevent this from happening, Barry uses a scrap of plywood held behind the fibreglass to protect the fabric from the drill.

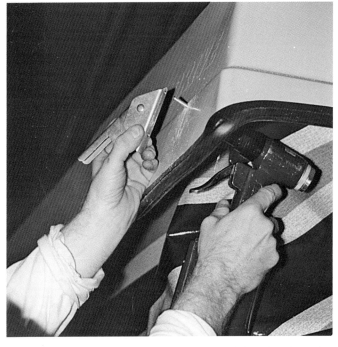

2-6-60. This time, again using a washer over the head of the rivet, the catch is riveted to the fibreglass panel with a rivet inserted from the inside of the elevating roof.

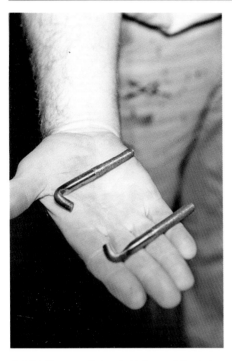

2-6-61. These are the two hold-down catches before fitting. Unfortunately, unlike the rest of the catch and clip assembly, they're in bare metal and need to be painted before fitting.

2-6-62. Each of these catches is threaded and is screwed into a female thread on the top part of the assembly. You'll need to adjust the position of the catch so that the elevating roof is pulled down tightly on its seal.
Important note: The seal will compress over time, and this will tend to leave the catch looser than it ought to be with the attendant risk of the elevating roof flying up when you are driving at speed. **Be sure to check the tightness of the catch at regular intervals and readjust it as the tension goes from the new rubber seal.**

2-6-63. Here's a most important point that must not be overlooked. To make certain that there are no leaks, both of the strut mountings, front and rear, need to be sealed with silicone sealant all the way around each mounting.

2-6-64. Similarly, the fabric must be sealed between the van body and the fabric itself.

2-6-65. More clear silicone sealant is used on each sewn seam on the fabric roof ...

2-6-66. ... including those on the pockets for the elevating roof frame. Basically, anywhere that has been stitched can leak and will need to be sealed.

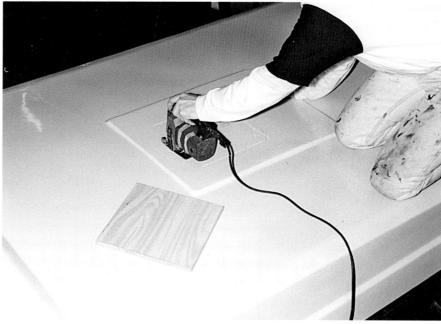

2-6-68. The fibreglass and timber are both cut through with the jigsaw.

2-6-67. Our motor caravan had a ventilator fitted to the roof. Barry marks the shape and size of the cut-out with a pencil using a template, positioning it symmetrically over the wooden insert included in the fibreglass roof.

SAFETY FIRST!

- It is **essential** that you wear an efficient face mask when drilling or sawing fibreglass.
- Fibreglass dust is potentially extremely injurious to health.

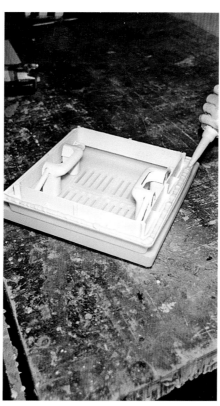

2-6-69. Sealer is applied to the vent where it will sit on the roof ...

2-6-70. ... and the vent is offered up onto the now-open elevating top.

2-6-71. While someone holds the outer part of the vent in place on the outside, the inner trim is pushed into place on the inside of the roof and screwed to the outer section of the vent, sandwiching the roof between them.

2-6-72. The completed roof on our Syncro Caravelle in Leisuredrive's workshop. We've had several years of use of the vehicle since this shot was taken and we haven't experienced one single drip of water coming in from the outside.

SECTION 7. FITTING AN ELEVATING ROOF TO A T4 TRANSPORTER

In some respects - particularly to do with reinforcing and strengthening - fitting an elevating roof to the T4 Transporter follows the approach described for the T4 high-top in Section 5, so it may be useful to refer to that section too.

2-7-1. Make sure that any wiring is moved safely out of the way. This is the wiring to the central interior light.

2-7-2. More wiring runs down the side of the van and this also needs to be carefully removed. If it needs to be reused, disconnect it at its source and feed it back through the panels, being sure to label all of the connections so that they can be remade correctly later - you'll be sure to forget!

2-7-3. Barry Roberts drills a hole in the roof to mark the position tight against the roof bars where he will start cutting on the outside of the roof.

2-7-4. Barry then drills more holes around the perimeter of the strengthening bars so that when he cuts the roof away, he'll be cutting inboard of the strengthening bars. Note that he'll also have to cut out bracing struts that run across the roof of the van where necessary. For those who have never done this before, it will be necessary to refer to the Leisuredrive replacement strengthening bars to see exactly where the cutting needs to take place.

2-7-5. Barry uses a straight edge on the outside of the roof to join-the-dots.

2-7-6. Barry has to kneel on the roof itself to make the front cut across the cab so, for that reason, this is the first cut that he makes so that he can be sure to be kneeling on the strength of the cross-bracing. It's a bit like removing a branch from a tree; you don't stand on the one you're going to cut off!

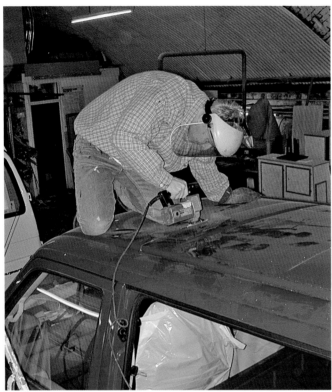

2-7-7. Barry continues the cut along the width of the roof ...

2-7-8. ... until he reaches the end of the cut line where he goes round the bend, so to speak, easing the jigsaw through a curved arc - he can go back later and square up the corner after completing the cut.

2-7-9. As you can see, the cuts that run along the edges and across the back of the van can be done while standing on a pair of steps.

2-7-10. As each corner comes loose, Barry props it up with a piece of wood across the corner - this roof section is heavier than that on the T3 because of the extra size and the amount of ribbing built into it.

2-7-11. With the three cut corners of the roof supported, Barry completes the cut into the final corner of the roof.

2-7-12. The cut-out roof panel can be slid carefully over the side of the van but great care has to be taken not to damage the van's paintwork.

2-7-13. It takes both Barrys combined to lift the redundant roof section away from the van.

Top tip!
• If you're not used to carrying out this work, it would be advisable to protect the sides of the van with old blankets to reduce the risk of causing any damage as the heavy roof section is removed.

2-7-14. Barry cleans up all the way around the edge of the cut-out roof with a file to remove any rough edges before painting the bare metal with primer.

2-7-15. These Volkswagen-approved strengthening sections are essential when it comes to restoring rigidity to the van. This is the Leisuredrive replacement rear crossmember.

2-7-16. At the front, the strengthening section is even more impressively substantial because that's where the extra strength needs to be.

2-7-17. The rear section is fitted to the van top after drilling suitable sized holes using a series of strong pop rivets.

2-7-18. You could also, as a belt-and-braces measure, use a bonding material such as Wurth Bond & Seal which is best used with a primer for treating the surfaces to be bonded together.

2-7-19. A further cut has to be made to the front section of the roof but only after the front reinforcing panel has been fitted.

2-7-20. Here you can see the front reinforcing section having been fitted to the roof, which has then allowed the shape to be transferred to the roof panel and once again a cut made using the jigsaw.

2-7-21. Barry fits the edge reinforcing and finishing member to the right-hand side of the roof first.

2-7-22. On the other side of the roof, the reinforcing panel has the wiring, which you saw being removed earlier in this section, running behind it. Barry fits the wiring into position on the reinforcing section ...

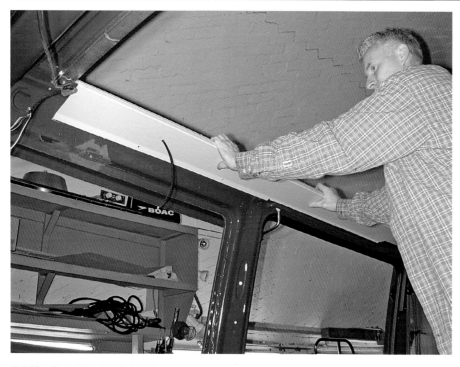

2-7-23. ... before locating the section on the inside of the roof and in conjunction with each of the reinforcing sections already fitted, front and rear.

2-7-24. The same process of bonding and pop riveting is carried out to fit this panel into place.

2-7-25. At the front, a finisher panel tidies up the corner where the side panel meets the crossmember.

2-7-26. Now it's over to the Leisuredrive GRP shop where an elevating roof top has been made, and can be seen being brought out of the mould in amongst all the other fibreglass panels that the operatives are busy making.

2-7-27. The elevating roof shell has been removed from the mould and trimmed, and is now being carried to the van ready to be fitted.

2-7-28. You'll need to take great care when lifting the elevating roof on to the van so as not to cause any damage to the paintwork. Leisuredrive has already fitted the hinges and the catches to the van's steelwork, having used templates to determine their exact correct position.

2-7-29. Hinges and catches could be fitted to the steelwork after the top had been placed in position - it's just slightly easier to reach both sides without the top on the vehicle.

2-7-30. Leisuredrive's MD Derek Andrews lends a hand by checking that the position of the top is precisely correct at the front corners.

2-7-31. Derek also checks the fit at the rear, before proceeding any further.

2-7-32. Derek risks life, limb and some things he doesn't like to think about, by sitting on the roof to hold it down tight while Barry drills the correct position for the catch at the rear of the roof.

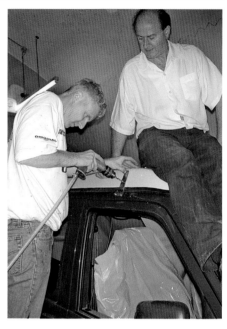

2-7-33. The pair now transfer their attention to the front of the roof where the front catch is similarly fitted.

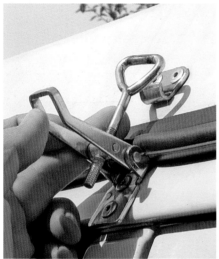

2-7-34. This is the catch assembly completely fitted into place.

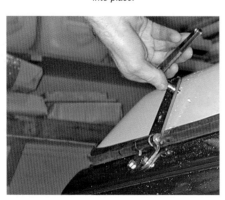

2-7-35. On the other side of the roof, the same treatment is meted out to the hinges. Positions are established by holding the roof down firmly and drilling, then bolts are inserted from the outside ...

2-7-36. ... while a nut and washer are applied and locked with a spanner on the inside.

2-7-37. Before fitting the elevating mechanism - see Section 6. Fitting an elevating roof to T3 Transporter - Derek measures the roof elevation to get it in precisely the correct position, holding it there with a wooden prop before starting on the elevator mechanism.

2-7-38. The handle for pulling the roof down again also has to be fitted to the inside of the roof. Refer to Section 6 - Fitting an elevating roof to T3 Transporter - for details of fitting the elevating roof struts.

2-7-39. This enables the roof to be pulled down against the force of the struts when closing the roof.

2-7-40. The Leisuredrive elevating roof gives more than enough headroom when raised, and a low roof line when it's not.

Chapter 3
Interior structural work

INTRODUCTION

This chapter is based around the Leisuredrive furniture units shown here. In principle, it also applies to any other types of units that you might use, including home-built ones. However, it's essential that you note the following:

• The Leisuredrive fitters shown here have great experience in fitting their own company's components, so there is a great sense of certainty about what-goes-where.
• Anyone fitting their own units will almost certainly be doing it for the first time.
• Even if you are fitting Leisuredrive units - but especially if you're not - you will need to follow extra measurement and location checks when carrying out the work.

Important note: Please read the introduction to Chapter 4: Gas, water and electricity before carrying out any of the work described in this chapter. Interiors and appliances can be like the chicken and the egg: it's not always obvious which comes first ...

FACT FILE: CUTTING HOLES IN BODY AND FLOOR

1. Don't cut holes in the floor or bodywork for units such as 'fridges, water heaters and space heaters (see Chapter 4) until you know precisely where they will be fitted.

Intro 1. No matter which interior layout you choose, you will still be able to choose between an elevating roof or one of the two styles of high-top for your conversion.

2. You can't easily know where they will be fitted until the furniture is in place.

3. But: You won't be able to fit some of these components with the furniture in place.

4. So: i) Fit the furniture temporarily.

ii) Establish the exact positions of the gas and electrical components and of the holes that will need to be cut. iii) Remove the furniture, as necessary, cut holes and fit any components that need to be fitted before the furniture. iv) Permanently fit the furniture.

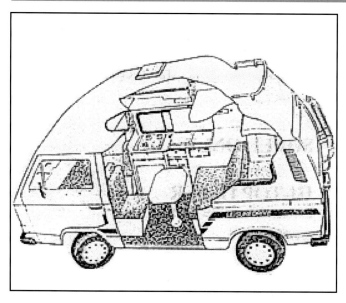

Intro 2. This is the classic Leisuredrive Crusader conversion used on the author's motor caravan, though with an elevating roof.

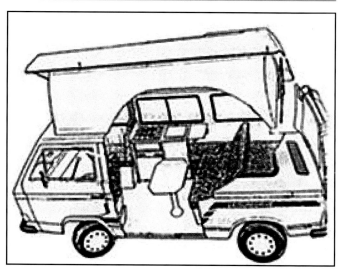

Intro 3. This is the conversion that Leisuredrive calls its Daytime conversion with more of an emphasis on picnicking and day trips than lengthy stays away from home.

Intro 4. If you intend to take small children with you, it may be easier to erect the 'upstairs' beds and the interior will certainly be warmer in cool weather.

Intro 5. Because the engine is at the front on T4 Transporters, the under-bed area is used for storage, and is accessible through the rear doors. This conversion gives the maximum amount of space inside the motor caravan but leaves none of the boot space that you find in a T3 Transporter, except for that storage space beneath the bed.

Intro 6. The advantage of the set-back bed is the large amount of living space in the centre of the van.

Intro 7. An alternative conversion provides extra luggage carrying capacity ...

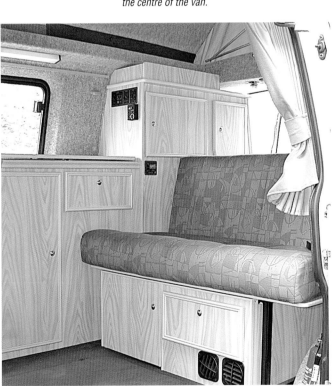

Intro 8. ... at the expense of space in the living room.

Intro 9. All conversions benefit from having a swivel passenger seat which is like adding one extra seat to the living space. And, if you have a row, you can always turn it to face the other way again!

SECTION 1. REMOVE TRIM AND WIRING

The following pictures and captions will guide you through the steps involved in this procedure.

3-1-1. This T4 van was once a plumber's van but all the inevitable build-up of dirt has been cleaned out from the inside ready to start work.

3-1-3. Put the fixing bolts back into their threaded holes for safe-keeping and lift out the seats ready for retrimming, if necessary, or store them safely for reuse later on.

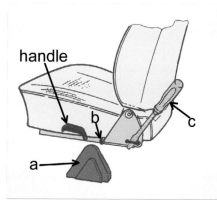

3-1-4. T3 seats come out in a different way. Lift the locking handle and slide the seat forward as far as it will go. Use a screwdriver to lever up the catch (b) then lift the handle again and slide the seat completely away from its runners. If you want to remove the backrest, you need to carefully pull off the plastic cover (a) and then use a screwdriver (c) to lever out the clip on the hinge plate that holds the backrest in place.

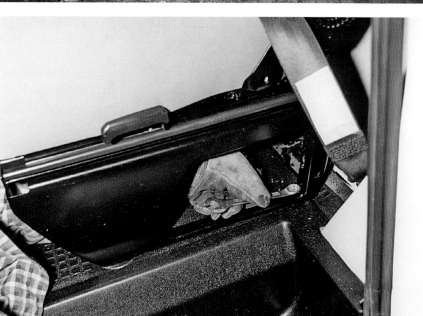

3-1-2. The seat bases are simply bolted down to the floor.

3-1-5. Interior trim on a T4 is held in place with a number of semi-concealed fixings. Many of them have a plug that looks like this placed over the fixing and all these plugs must be carefully levered off. Put them in a plastic bag so that you can reuse them later.

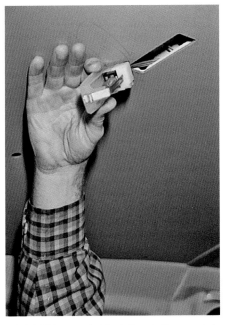

3-1-6. Make sure that the battery is disconnected and remove the interior lights.

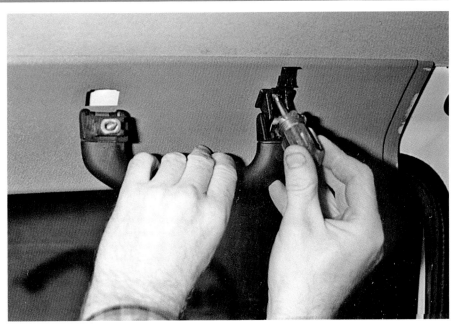

3-1-7. Unscrew and remove any grab handles that are fitted.

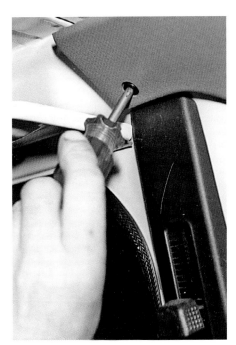

3-1-8. In some cases, there will be screws beneath the covers shown in Pic 5. Where applicable, unscrew them ...

3-1-9. ... and remove the relevant pieces of trim.

3-1-10. This trim strip, across the back of the cab, is carefully levered away.

3-1-11. The door opening trim is also held in place with screws which are found beneath the concealed caps shown earlier.

3-1-12. This trim is now free to be removed from above the door ...

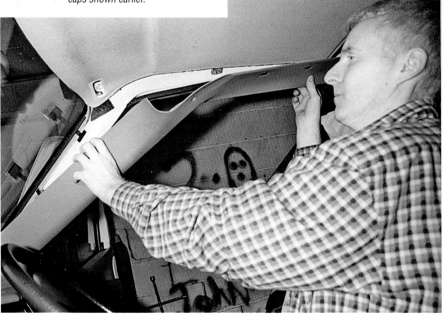

3-1-13. ... and can be unclipped from the windscreen A-pillar.

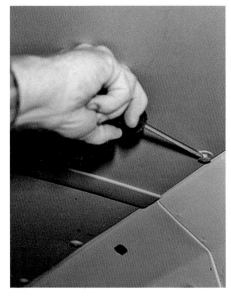

3-1-14. In some instances, headlining board is held in place with a different type of trim clip. This type has a central peg which is first carefully levered out a few millimetres.

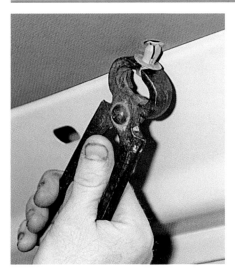

3-1-15. Leisuredrive's tip is now to use woodworker's pincers to pull the clip, complete with peg, out of the hole in the headlining.

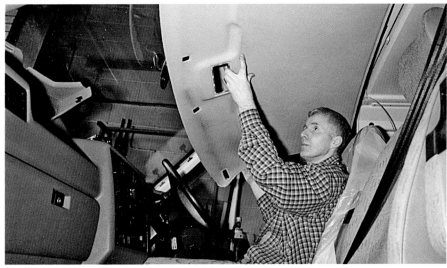

3-1-16. The front headlining is simply lowered from its position on the roof.

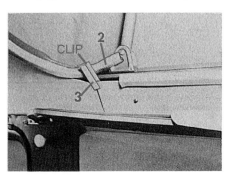

3-1-17. T3 headlining has to be removed after first levering up the finisher strip (2) and then sliding out the H-shaped trim clip (3) - this is only applicable to earlier versions.

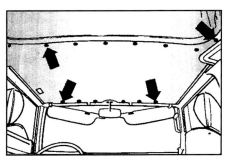

3-1-18. The headlining may then be held by a series of screws (arrowed), which are removed ...

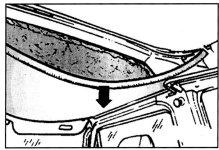

3-1-19. ... before flexing the headlining downwards, in the direction of the arrow and removing it from the vehicle.

3-1-20. T4 models may also have rear headlining which is removed in a similar way to that of the front cab headlining.

3-1-21. Before any of the cutting out can be done for the roof and windows, certain items of wiring need to be removed. This is the interior light operating switch on the T4's sliding door front pillar.

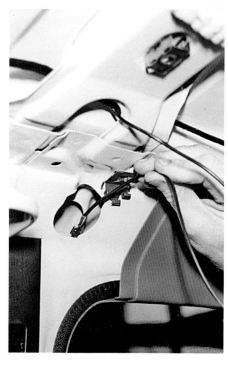

3-1-22. The wiring to the switch can now be pulled out of the pillar ...

3-1-23. ... and removed from the roof panel where necessary.

3-1-24. It's important to label each end of any disconnected wiring so that you will know where to refit it later. Use a piece of masking tape, wrap it around the end to form a tag and write an identifying number on it to match the same number on the piece of wire that must go into the connector.

SECTION 2. REMOVE T4 BULKHEAD PANEL

On many T4 vans, there is a bulkhead panel fitted behind the front seats and running right across the van. This must, of course, be removed before the conversion work can be commenced.

3-2-1. In this section we will show Leisuredrive's foreman Barry Roberts using an air chisel to cut away the bulkhead. If you are not experienced in carrying out this work, there may be some risk of damaging the van's outer panels and a better alternative would be this Clarke compressed air-powered panel saw. There will be a little bit more cleaning up to do with the angle grinder but a much reduced risk of causing damage. It will cut much closer to the edge of a panel than an electric jigsaw.

SAFETY FIRST!
• Always wear industrial-type protective gloves when cutting sheet metal.
• Always wear eye protection whenever using power tools for cutting metal.

3-2-2. Barry starts by cutting the top of the panel away from its mountings on the door pillar. The welded-on tabs of metal are left attached to the door pillar for now.

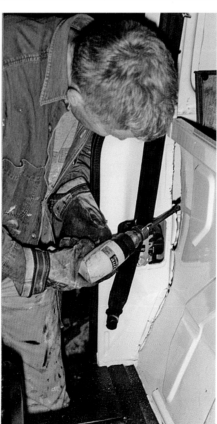

3-2-3. He now cuts down the length of the bulkhead panel from top to bottom.

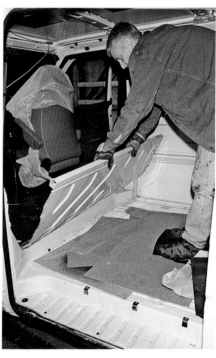

3-2-4. The panel can now be folded down into the back of the van.
NOTE: If you're not using an air chisel, don't fold the panel down: instead, use the saw to cut right across the panel from side to side.

3-2-5. Barry cuts the joint between the bulkhead panel and the floor.

3-2-6. The redundant bulkhead panel can now be lifted out of the vehicle.

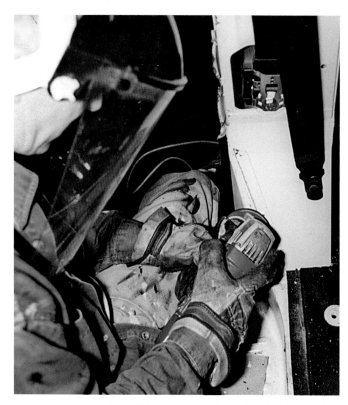

3-2-7. In some cases, there will be seams remaining on the vehicle held in place with spot welds. Use the angle grinder to grind carefully through each spot weld but taking great care not to cut into the panel beneath.

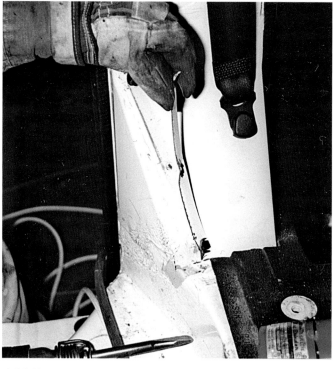

3-2-8. Use a screwdriver to lever the seam off the remnants of its spot weld and lift it away.

SECTION 3. FITTING REAR SEAT BELTS

If the van you are converting was designed as a people carrier, there may be rear seat belt mountings already fitted. However, it is extremely unlikely that they will be suitable for the converted van because of the special position of the rear seats on a motor caravan.

SAFETY FIRST!

• You must not attempt to make up your own seat belt mountings for the rear seats of your motor caravan.
• This section shows Leisuredrive fitting seat belt mountings to the rear of T3 and T4 VW Transporters but the positions and the fitting process are critical.
• For obvious safety reasons, this work must be entrusted to an experienced, approved specialist.

3-3-1. Leisuredrive's foreman Barry starts by checking the rear of the van to see whether there are any existing seat belt mountings in position and to determine the correct locations for the new ones.

3-3-2. Since my van was a Caravelle, some of the rear seat belt mountings that are already fitted could be reused. However, because there was going to be a kitchen unit along one side of the van, the seat belt on the right-hand side had to be a lap-only belt. There's no means of attaching the shoulder strap high enough on the van in a safe location.

3-3-3. Barry gently uses the angle grinder to remove all paint from the area where welding is to take place. It's best to use a sanding disc on a rubber backing pad.

3-3-4. On this T4 van, there is a mounting position but no mounting fitted. Barry bends the mounting plate forward and welds a nut onto the back of it.

3-3-5. He then folds it back into position and reinforces the plate before welding it securely to the bodywork. This bolt has been used to align the nut and to prevent weld spatter from getting into the threads while the welding takes place.

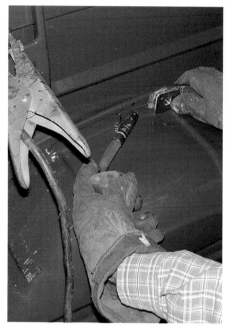

3-3-6. In this location, a nut-plate has to be welded onto the body after first drilling the box section to give room for the nut to be located.

3-3-7. An alternative method used in this location on a T3 is a thick threaded plate which Barry welds to the body.

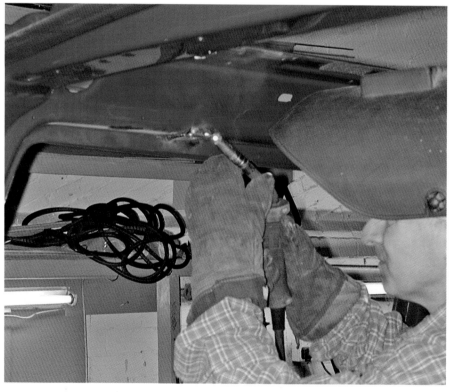

3-3-8. On this T4 Transporter, a similar plate is welded to the roof frame ...

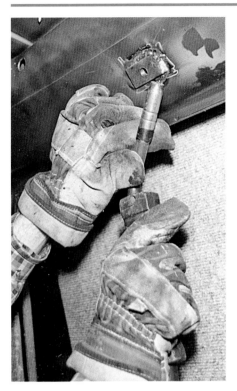

3-3-9. ... and this is a similar version being welded to a T3 Transporter. Once again, Barry had to pre-drill a hole in the rail to allow the fixing bolt to pass through.

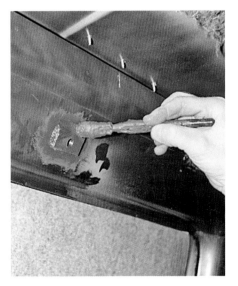

3-3-10. Finally, the new mounting is painted to prevent it from rusting. Bear in mind that any wax protection will have been burned off the inside of all welds, and fresh wax will need to be injected behind each mounting point where welding has taken place.

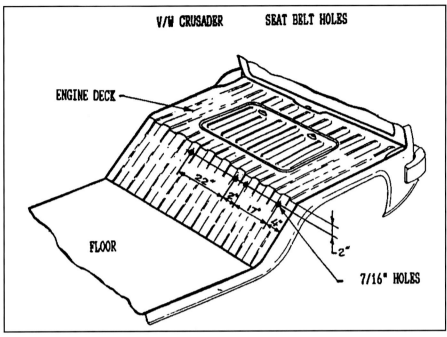

3-3-11. Where no mounting points exist, these are the dimensions used by Leisuredrive for fitting mounting points to the floor of a T3 model.

SAFETY FIRST!

• All seat belt mountings must be carried out to an approved standard and only by a qualified welder.
• Seat belt mountings must be to a manufacturer's original specification.
• You are strongly recommended to ONLY have your local VW dealer, Leisuredrive or other properly qualified workshop fit new seat belt mountings.

SECTION 4. FITTING ROOF LOCKER

Note that part of the job of fitting the roof locker on elevating roof models is so connected with trim that part of this process is described in Section 5, Interior panels and wall coverings.

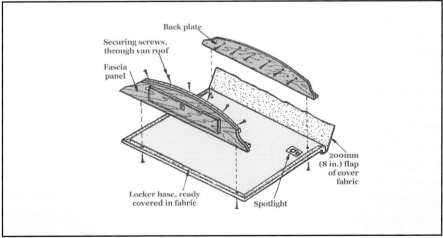

3-4-1. This is the roof locker for elevating roof models. The reason that the locker fascia can be screwed through the van roof is, of course, because the elevating roof fits over the top, so you will be screwing through a sealed area. This is not something that you should do with any of the high-top roof models!

3-4-2. If you're not buying a kit, you will need to cut out a fascia panel to the exact profile of the van roof. This might take some trial and error and will best be done by making a cardboard template first.

3-4-3. In the case of a high-top roof, there may be a fascia panel which is fitted to a locker at the rear of the van. In this case, the panel is screwed to bearers built in to the fibreglass. In these cases it is also important to trim the interior of the locker before fitting the fascia panel.

3-4-5. IMPORTANT NOTE: If you intend fitting spot lights or speakers to any part of the roof locker, make sure that you do so before the panels are fitted to the vehicle. Access could be extremely difficult otherwise.

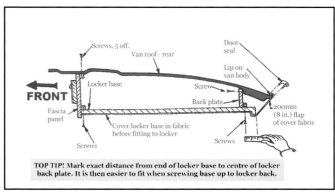

3-4-4. This helps to describe the way in which the locker will be fitted to the vehicle. Note that the fascia panel is screwed on first and that the remainder is fitted as described in the next section.

3-4-6. This is the roof locker fascia fitted to the roof of an elevating roof conversion, prior to fitting the rest of the roof locker.

SECTION 5. INTERIOR PANELS AND WALL COVERINGS

The following pictures and captions will guide you through the steps involved in this procedure.

SAFETY FIRST!

• Always wear protective gloves and a breathing mask when handling fibreglass. The particles can be harmful to health.
• Work in a well-ventilated area when working with impact trim adhesive. Be sure to follow the safety notes supplied with the product.

3-5-1. Take this one-off opportunity to insulate all of the wall cavities. Fibreglass loft insulation will be fine provided that you don't use it in places where water can get in, such as inside doors with wind-down windows, because it will hold water and cause corrosion.

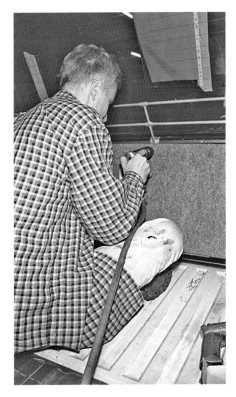

3-5-2. A new tailgate panel has been made out of hardboard and trimmed in the same cloth to be used for the rest of the vehicle's interior. You could either use the original fixing clips for holding the panel in place, or drill fresh holes and use self-tapping screws.

3-5-3. In several places, new trim will have to be glued down to painted metalwork. Barry Roberts has wiped all such panels with spirit wipe to remove any grease and is now lightly sanding the surface to help the glue grip better.

3-5-4. The cloth that Leisuredrive uses for the interior trim has a great deal of stretch. Where it is glued down to curved surfaces, such as around the glass area on this Caravelle sliding door, the cloth has to be stretched and also pushed down into concave areas. Barry uses the handle-end of a pair of scissors to press the cloth down firmly into tight concaves.

3-5-5. Here, over a door, Barry has already glued down the top part of the cloth and is now applying aerosol adhesive where the cloth will cover the rail above the door aperture.

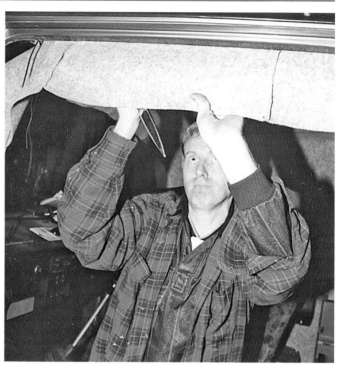

3-5-6. The cloth is pulled evenly but reasonably taut and glued down around the rail.

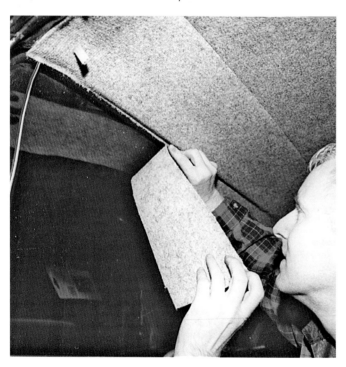

3-5-7. When the glue has dried sufficiently to hold the cloth in place, Barry cuts off the surplus ready for the door seal to be fitted later. This particular piece of cloth is the outer edge of the front headlining.

3-5-8. In the back of the van, the walls need to be trimmed to give a smooth surface. This is something best done in stages, trying to get the height and (on a T3 Transporter), the fit around the engine bay right as a first step.

3-5-9. The length can be marked out by drawing around the shape of the door opening. Note that any apertures needed for items such as seat belts will also have to be cut into the panel at this stage.

3-5-10. Barry takes the marked-out panels off the van and over to his workbench where he cuts them out with a power jigsaw.

3-5-11. Once the panels are correctly shaped, they can be screwed to the strengthening ribs. Take care not to use over-long screws because they will damage the outer skin on the van.

3-5-12. Barry starts to fit the cloth trim to the inside of the van by first cutting the cloth roughly to shape and then applying adhesive along the top of the van side. Note that no adhesive is applied lower down at this stage.

3-5-13. The cloth is offered up and pushed into position, using the 'shuffling-time' allowed by the glue before it dries and sets.

3-5-14. Barry uses the handle of his scissors to make sure that the cloth is fitted correctly to the shape of the rail at the top of the side panel.

3-5-15. He now moves on to glue the cloth further down, just beneath the line of the windows.

3-5-16. Barry works down the panel, gluing the cloth to the lower hardboard sheet as he goes.

3-5-17. Cut-outs will need to be made in certain positions, such as around the sliding door mechanism and seat belt mountings.

3-5-18. As each of the trim panels is fitted into place, you may wish to fit items such as the seat belt mountings and other objects that will be screwed on through the trim to hold it firmly in place.

3-5-19. Note the position of this thin wooden strip which is screwed to the hollow-section around the inside of the van, just above the window and door apertures. We'll come back to what this strip is for in just a moment.

3-5-20. Now working at the rear of the roof, Barry continues to measure, check and cut his trim materials accordingly. Note the way in which electric cables which need to pass across the roof have been taped into position to hold them in place while the trim is fixed.

3-5-21. Barry applies spray-on adhesive to the inside of the trim cloth this time. You have to take very great care not to concentrate the adhesive too heavily in one position otherwise it will show through as a yellow stain. Try holding the can a little way away from the cloth so that the adhesive has started to dry before it hits the surface of the cloth.

3-5-22. Barry uses that shuffling time again to stretch the cloth into position making sure that there are no creases. He works from the centre-outwards in each direction.

3-5-23. Here, on the other side of the van, the surplus can now be cut away.

3-5-24. Cloth is stretched downwards across the opening and Barry staples it to the strip of timber screwed on previously.

3-5-25. The same procedure is carried out on the other side of the van, again making sure that the tension is even and that there are no creases in the cloth.

3-5-26. You constantly have to be aware of positions where cables may need to protrude through the headlining, such as for the interior strip light in this position.

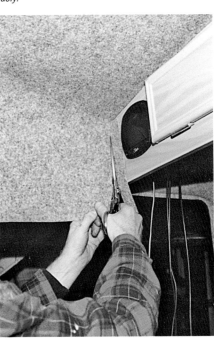

3-5-27. Where the trim is fitted against the locker fascia, Barry carefully cuts it to give a neat edge.

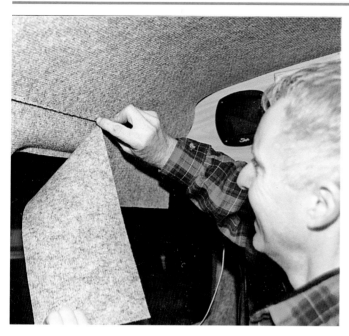

3-5-28. A sharp knife blade is used to cut the cloth level with the bottom of the timber strip we showed being fitted earlier.

3-5-29. This is the piece of cloth that will stretch from the opening in the roof down to the van sidewalls. Barry starts by gluing it in place around the roof opening.

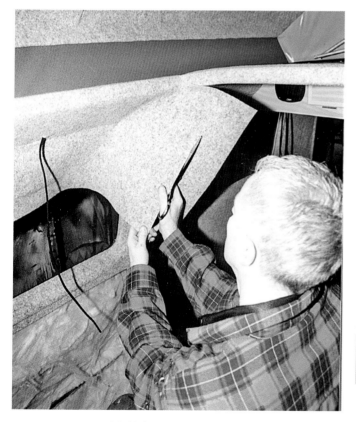

3-5-30. Surplus cloth is cut away.

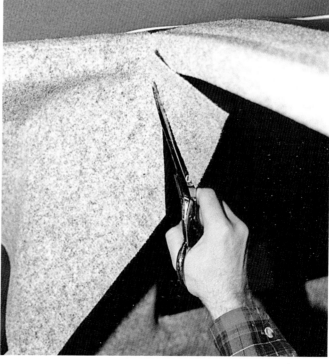

3-5-31. Note that it's best to cut away surplus in stages. It's very difficult to gauge the correct amount in one go and far better to cut off too little rather than too much.

3-5-32. Where the cloth trim that Barry has just fitted covers the edge of the material shown being fitted in Pic 28, the surplus material is folded over to produce a seam.

3-5-33. With the seam tucked neatly in, the edge of the fabric is stapled down to the same wooden strip and trimmed off in the same way as before.

3-5-34. In Section 4, we mentioned that the roof locker on elevating roof models is best fitted along with the trim. Barry points out the relatively large amount of wiring that comes into this area because of the location of the electrical unit and fan controller on the wardrobe.

3-5-35. A piece of trim cloth is cut over-size, as before, and offered up to make sure it fits the space inside what will become the locker.

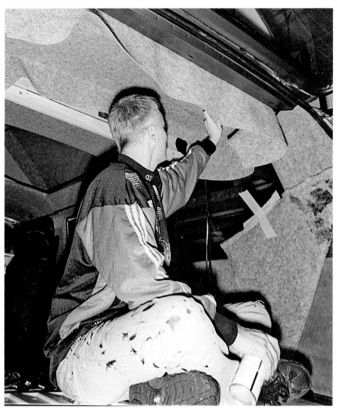

3-5-36. The cloth is glued down with spray adhesive, as before, stretched, fitted and then trimmed off where necessary.

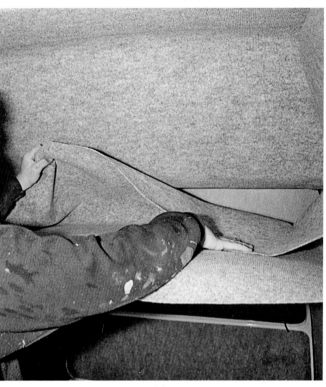

3-5-37. The other Barry trims the locker space in a high-top conversion. The principles of doing so are the same as for the rest of the interior, and it's necessary to trim this area before any locker fascias are fitted.

3-5-38. This is the locker base plate and Barry cuts a piece of trim sufficient in size to fit the base plate and wrap around the edges.

3-5-39. The base plate is turned over and the trim cloth glued down leaving the surface on the visible side smooth and wrinkle-free.

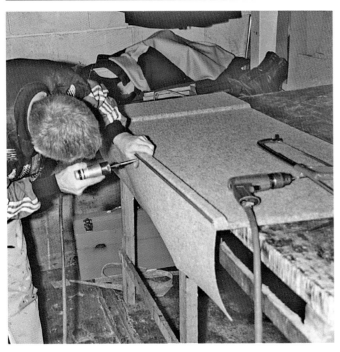

3-5-40. Note the flap of material that has to be left hanging free over the edge of the base plate - see Section 4, Pic 1. With a typical bit of forward planning, Barry fits the curtain rail to the timber strip on the back of the locker panel. It's so much easier to get at now!

3-5-41. It takes two to offer up the locker base panel.

3-5-42. With the panel held precisely in position, it can be screwed in as described in Section 4.

3-5-43. Barry uses spray adhesive on the rear of the base plate and the edge of the tailgate opening.

3-5-44. The flap of cloth is glued down ...

3-5-45. ... right up to the edge of the door opening.

3-5-46. The sealing strip can be tapped in place back on to the door opening, starting at the top ...

3-5-47. ... and working down each side. Make sure that the strip goes over the finishing material and doesn't cause it to bunch as it pushes it off the steelwork.

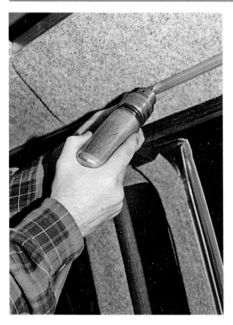

3-5-48. That strip of wood we mentioned earlier is used to screw the curtain rail in place, and the curtain rail is strategically placed so that it hides the cut edge of the fabric.

3-5-50. If the seats are now refitted, you can drive the van if you need to - but be sure to protect seats and trim from damage - your vehicle is no longer 'just' a van!

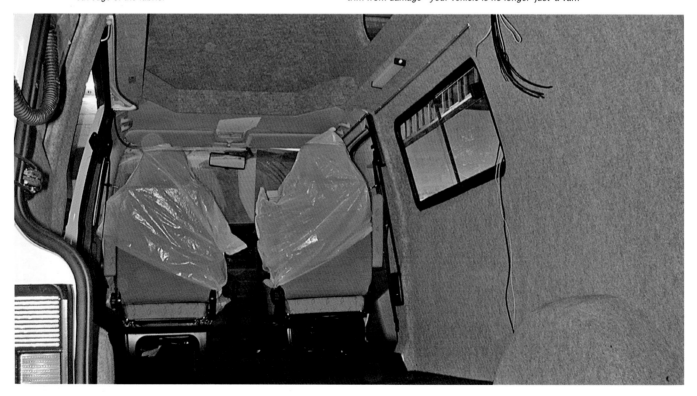

3-5-49. The floor and wall coverings are seen complete on this T4 van. Note that wiring is in place, as are interior lights and curtain track, but the roof locker has not yet been fitted.

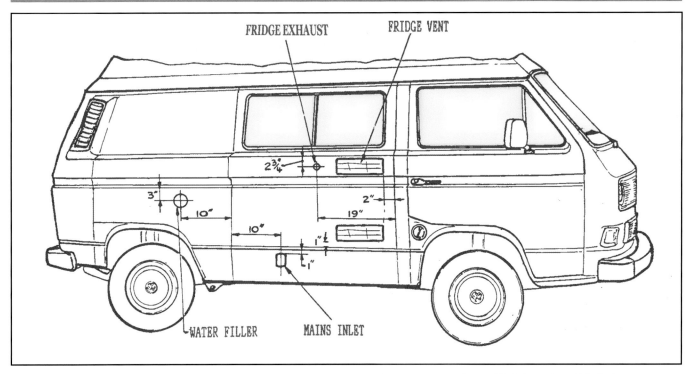

FRIDGE EXHAUST   FRIDGE VENT

WATER FILLER   MAINS INLET

3-6-1. Obviously, the number of holes you will need to cut, and their positions, will depend upon the accessories you'll be fitting to the vehicle. For instance, on our T3 Transporter, the water inlet hole is fitted into the recess in the pressing in the panel for a fuel filler hole, which was not used, on the left-hand side of the vehicle. It all depends on which side of the vehicle you site the water tank and the location of the base vehicle's fuel filler cap - positions vary and ours was different because the vehicle is a Syncro 4x4 model. Similarly, the location and number of flue or fridge vent holes you will need will depend on the type of unit you are fitting.

SECTION 6. FIT FLOOR AND CUT HOLES

The following pictures and captions will guide you through the steps involved in this procedure.

3-6-2. From the cost point of view, chipboard is the cheapest type of floor covering but plywood gives a better strength-to-weight ratio. If you use marine ply it will also be far less rot-prone and that would be the best, though most expensive, option.

3-6-3. It might be worth considering fitting the wall and side trims before fitting the floor, depending on whether or not you want the trim to be concealed behind the floorboards. Alternatively, the trim could be tucked behind floor coverings.

3-6-4. If possible, you should avoid drilling too many holes in the floor, and that includes holes for self-tapping screws. For that reason, the best way of holding floor panels down is to use a bonding agent.

3-6-5. Note that on our Caravelle, the original floor insulation material was retained and placed beneath the floorboards. Note the cut-outs in the insulation for the new rear seat belts.

3-6-6. Leisuredrive's Steve applies adhesive to the rear of each floorboard before gluing it down to the floor of the van.

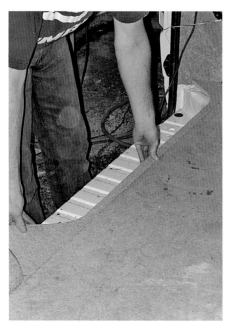

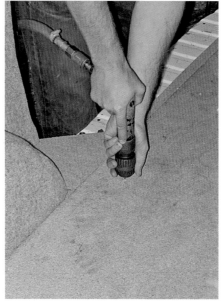

3-6-7. On this T4 van, part of the floorboards have to be cut to allow for the shape of the recessed step by the sliding door.

3-6-8. In this instance, the floorboard can be screwed down to a hollow box section without exposing it to the elements beneath. The board and the steel beneath are drilled ...

3-6-9. ... and screwed down to the floor.

3-6-10. The floorboards also act as the floor inside the cupboard units, so Steve glues down a piece of vinyl domestic floor covering to the area where the cupboard units will be fitted.

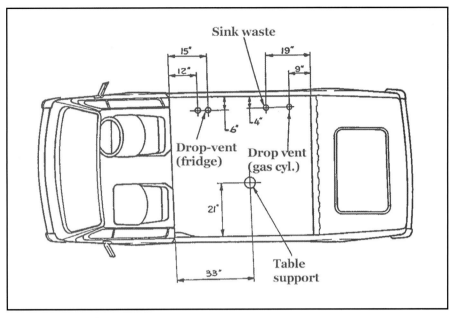

3-6-11. Unfortunately, you can't use this drawing as a template for the holes to be drilled in your vehicle because of the differences between base vehicles and components to be fitted. However, you should make a similar plan to this one showing exactly where all holes will need to go. Not only will you have to bear in mind the shape and size of the accessories being fitted, but also the shape of the van's chassis rails and, most importantly, fuel and brake lines, electrical cables, mounting points and other components fitted to the underside of the vehicle.

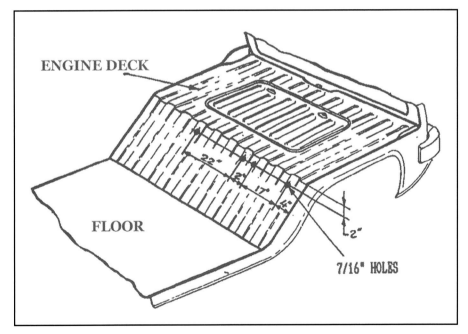

3-6-12. This is another example of a plan made for holes to be drilled, including those in the rear deck where a Propex heater is being fitted. In the case of our van, a Propex heater of a different design to the one allowed for here was fitted, which just goes to emphasise the need for tailoring each van's requirements to the components you will be fitting.

3-6-13. A case in point is this Belling Mallaga E water storage heater. Steve works out the exact positions inside the cupboard units and establishes the correct location for the heater. See Chapter 4 for further fitting information.

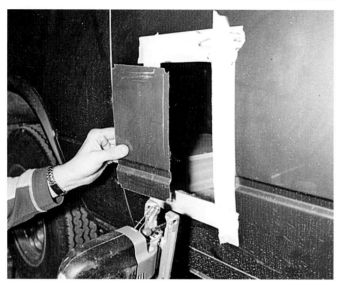

3-6-14. Quite a hair-raising moment, so you don't want to get it wrong! A hole is cut in the side of the van for the Mallaga E. Fortunately, Belling provides a cutting template along with the fitting instructions. No-one from Belling will come and measure its correct location for you, however, so that's something you have to be absolutely sure about.

3-6-15. After consulting the instructions for the Propex blown-air heater, Steve drills holes in the floor for the exhaust and for the vents.

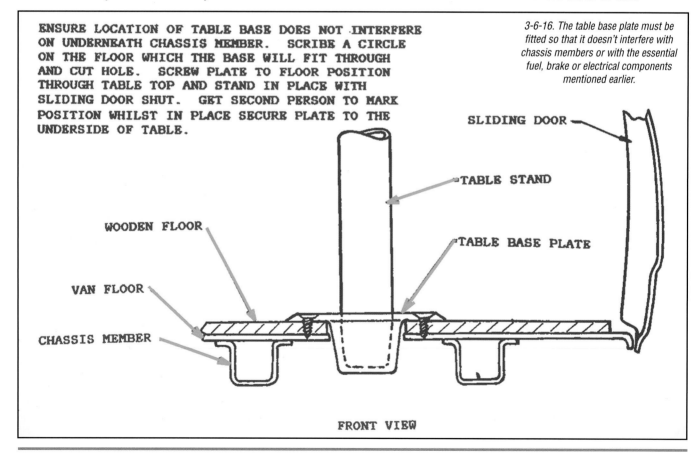

ENSURE LOCATION OF TABLE BASE DOES NOT INTERFERE ON UNDERNEATH CHASSIS MEMBER. SCRIBE A CIRCLE ON THE FLOOR WHICH THE BASE WILL FIT THROUGH AND CUT HOLE. SCREW PLATE TO FLOOR POSITION THROUGH TABLE TOP AND STAND IN PLACE WITH SLIDING DOOR SHUT. GET SECOND PERSON TO MARK POSITION WHILST IN PLACE SECURE PLATE TO THE UNDERSIDE OF TABLE.

3-6-16. The table base plate must be fitted so that it doesn't interfere with chassis members or with the essential fuel, brake or electrical components mentioned earlier.

SLIDING DOOR

TABLE STAND

TABLE BASE PLATE

WOODEN FLOOR

VAN FLOOR

CHASSIS MEMBER

FRONT VIEW

3-6-18. He paints the edges of the hole with metal primer to protect it against corrosion.

3-6-17. Using Leisuredrive's own fitting handbook, Steve measures the exact location for the table base plate before drilling a hole in the floor.

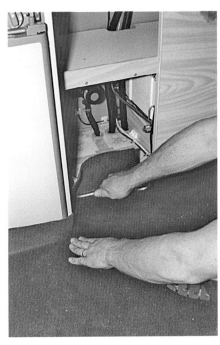

3-6-20. We've leapt ahead now to the point where the kitchen units have been fitted but before the bed base is in place. Roy Broadbent places the carpet in position and creases it down into the corners with the end of his scissors.

3-6-19. Meanwhile, back in the recesses of the Leisuredrive workshop, the carpet to go in the rear of the van has been marked out from a template and is being cut out slightly oversize.

3-6-21. The crease mark, clearly shown on the back of the carpet, can now be used to cut along so that the carpet fits properly.

3-6-22. There's more fiddly work involved around the fridge, where the carpet has to be tucked into place under the fridge body and also cut to fit the cabinet around the fridge.

3-6-23. Roy applies spray adhesive and glues the carpet to the floorboard area where the bed base will later be fitted.

3-6-24. The locations where gas bottles will be located and where the Propex heater will be fitted both need to have floor vents, and these can be fitted in place after the carpet has gone down, but not before.

3-6-25. The table base plate can also be fitted once the carpet in is place, screwing it right through the carpet and into the floorboard beneath.

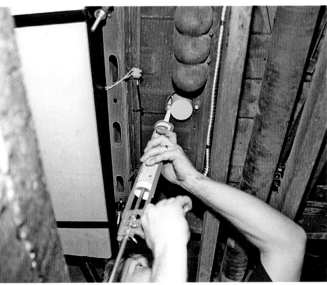

3-6-26. From beneath the vehicle, Roy applies sealer all the way around the underside of the table base plate so no moisture can get in between base plate and the floor of the vehicle.

3-6-28. These fibreglass door steps are from Leisuredrive. This one is cut off to length ...

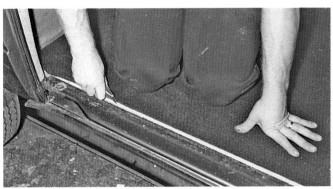

3-6-27. The carpet is trimmed back to the edge of the floorboard at the door opening.

3-6-29. ... before being glued and screwed down, with an edging strip covering the gap between door step and carpet.

SECTION 7. BUILDING THE FURNITURE

If you have specific needs and sufficient skill, you may, of course, wish to build your own furniture. Do be aware that unless you are able to work to professional standards, the interior of your van will not look professional, and its value, as well as its aesthetic appeal, will be reduced.

3-7-1. This is one of the Leisuredrive furniture kits available for the T4 Transporter. Some DIY converters choose to have the vehicle top fitted and the interior trim put in place so that their van looks like the one shown at the end of Section 5, and then to purchase the kit shown here from Leisuredrive (or one similar to it), and fit it themselves.

3-7-2. This is the same kit with the bed folded down. Each of the cabinets will be stiffer once fitted to the vehicle than it is here, so the kit is fitted with temporary stiffening struts which have to be removed as the kit is fitted.

Right: 3-7-3. Roy follows the Leisuredrive procedure for building one of the cupboard units.

Left: 3-7-4. Glue and screws are used along with timber batons to secure the laminated panels to each other.

3-7-5. The completed cupboard is made ready for assembly to the vehicle.

3-7-6. On this cupboard door opening, hot glue is applied ...

3-7-7. ... before edging strip is glued into place.

3-7-8. Staples are powered into the edging strip to add a belt to the braces.

3-7-9. This cupboard is also fitted with a door with an opening stay. Hinges and stays need to be fixed with special coarse-thread chipboard screws, otherwise they will quickly pull out.

3-7-10. Where a unit fits up against the side-wall, the edges are trimmed in fabric with one side folded under to produce a neat seam.

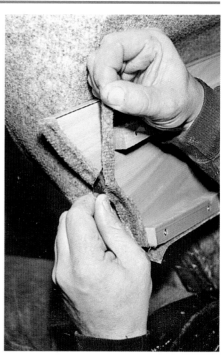

3-7-11. Surplus fabric is trimmed off the back of the panel.

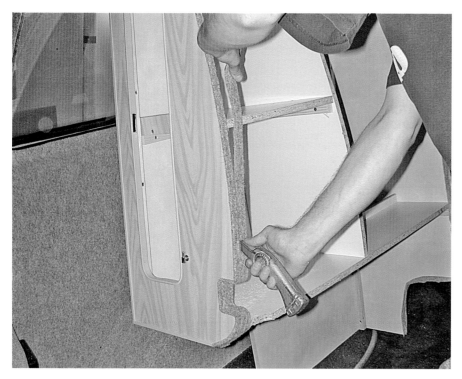

3-7-12. The previous shots showed the edging strip being fitted to a roof locker, but the same applies to the inner edge of a wardrobe unit where it will be fitted against the wall of the van.

3-7-13. The position of this single-post table support is carefully measured ...

3-7-14. ... before being screwed into position on the bottom of the table.

SECTION 8. KITCHEN UNIT

After the roof locker, the first major piece of furniture to be fitted is the kitchen unit because that's the one that connects to so many other services. As we said at the start of this chapter, it's important to work out the location of the kitchen unit in relation to those services and you may need to temporarily fit the kitchen unit and other furniture units in order to establish where the service components are going to go. You may then have to remove the kitchen unit, fit some of the services, such as a blown air heater or water heater, and then add the kitchen unit to the vehicle.

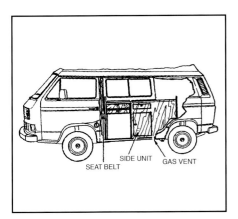

3-8-1. This shot indicates just some of the constraints around which the siting of the kitchen unit must be based. You have to consider the equipment fitted to the vehicle, such as seat belts, and 'non-negotiable' fittings for the services, such as the gas vent shown here.

3-8-2. Roy fits the CAK water tank to the underside of our Transporter Camper before fitting any of the units. In this way, he can work out the necessary access points for the water filler and water supply to the tap.

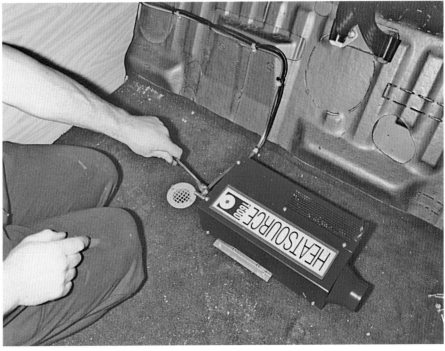

3-8-3. Similarly, the Propex heatsource warm air blower is fitted before the furniture for this part of the van is put into place.

3-8-4. The kitchen unit is ready assembled with hob, grill and sink unit before fitting it to the vehicle. Some of the electrical wiring, such as that for the fridge and the pipes for the gas hob, have also been fitted at this stage.

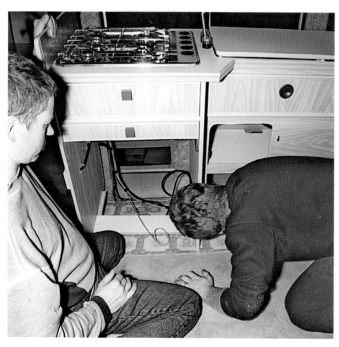

3-8-6. ... taking great care that it lines up with the items already fitted, such as the Mallaga E water heater which Roy is checking for correct location.

3-8-5. The unit is carefully manoeuvred into place ...

3-8-7. On some conversions, it may be necessary to cut part of a unit to fit around a wheelarch.

3-8-8. Although you will mark the cut-out required, it's best to take off too little than too much and to trim a little bit more off later if necessary. Alternatively, you could make a cardboard template, trimming it with a pair of scissors until the fit is perfect and then tracing around the template onto the unit.

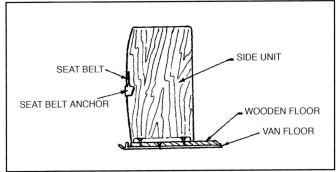

3-8-9. On some conversion styles, it may be necessary to trim the end of the unit to match seat belt mountings.

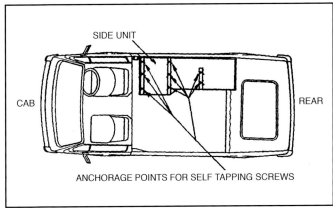

3-8-10. With Leisuredrive units, provision will have been made for screwing the unit to the floor by including timber batons in the unit's construction.

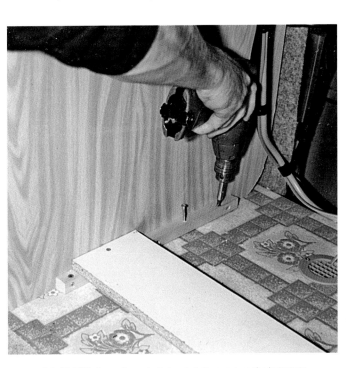

3-8-11. With the unit precisely located, Roy screws the batons to the floor ...

3-8-12. ... and then removes the bracing strut which had been put in place earlier to prevent distortion while the unit was being manhandled into the van.

3-8-13. This filler strip has been made to go down the edge of the unit to provide a draught strip between the unit's edge and the fridge.

3-8-14. Roy screws it to the edge of the panel. When choosing wood screws, be sure to allow for the fact that the screws will be countersunk so that you avoid the risk of the point of the screw breaking through the other side of the laminate.

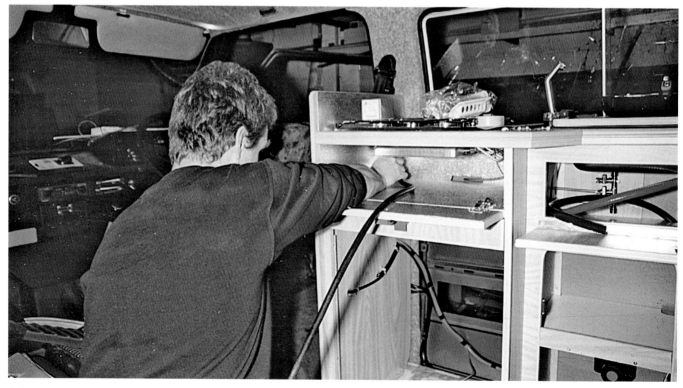

3-8-15. The top of the unit is secured to the wall of the van at the position of hollow box sections. Take care that the screws don't protrude too far and cause damage to the van's outer panels.

SECTION 9. WARDROBE AND TABLE STORE

For information on fitting the table support to the vehicle floor see Section 11. Fitting the table support.

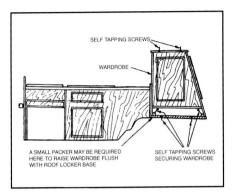

3-9-1. With the kitchen unit in place, the wardrobe unit can now be added. Note that, on an elevating roof conversion, the aim is to get the wardrobe unit top against the top of the van, using a packing piece at the base if necessary to raise the unit and fill any gap.

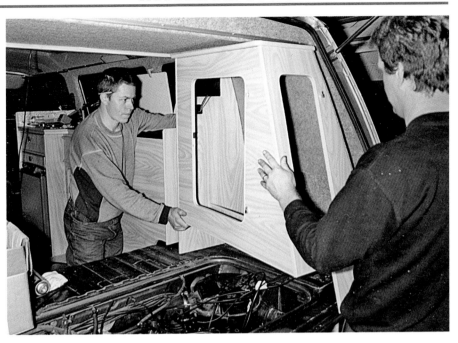

3-9-2. Steve and Roy manoeuvre the wardrobe unit into place, feeding the cables that are coming down from the roof into the wardrobe space.

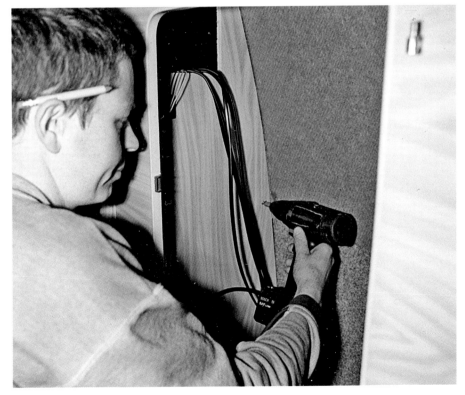

3-9-3. With the wardrobe located tight against the van roof and up against the kitchen unit, Steve screws the wardrobe into position against the kitchen unit.

3-9-4. At the rear of the unit, he uses angle brackets to screw the wardrobe to the sidewall of the van. It's not possible to use wooden batons here because of the curvature of the van wall.

3-9-5. In a high-top conversion, such as this T4, the wardrobe doesn't go tight up against the roof but needs to be fitted against the kitchen unit and level.

3-9-6. Roy checks the unit for position and also makes sure that the base of the unit is properly located on the floor. This is more critical on T4 models where, of course, there is no engine compartment.

3-9-7. As with the T3 model, the front of the wardrobe is screwed to the kitchen unit.

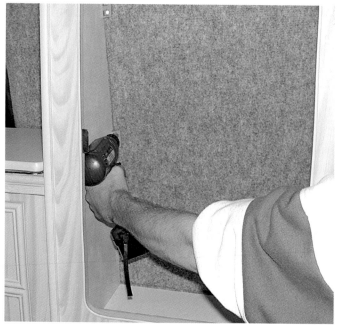

3-9-8. The wardrobe is also screwed to suitable mountings on the van wall, again using angle brackets.

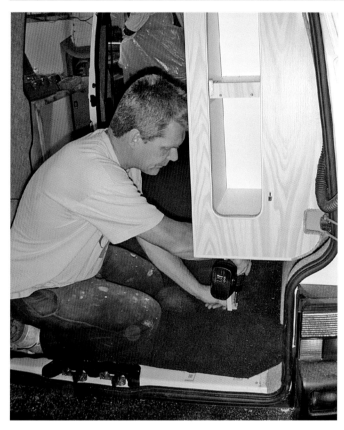

3-9-9. More brackets are used to hold the base of the wardrobe unit to the floor.

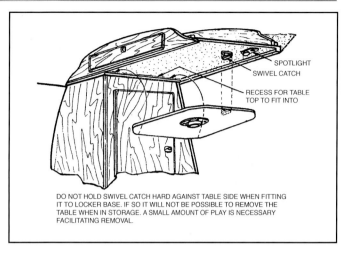

SPOTLIGHT

SWIVEL CATCH

RECESS FOR TABLE
TOP TO FIT INTO

DO NOT HOLD SWIVEL CATCH HARD AGAINST TABLE SIDE WHEN FITTING
IT TO LOCKER BASE. IF SO IT WILL NOT BE POSSIBLE TO REMOVE THE
TABLE WHEN IN STORAGE. A SMALL AMOUNT OF PLAY IS NECESSARY
FACILITATING REMOVAL.

3-9-10. Leisuredrive's favoured location for storing the table top is to stow it on
the ceiling, on the base of the locker unit.

3-9-11. The table top is held in its slot and the position for the fixing catch is
marked on the ceiling.

3-9-12. A block slightly thicker than the table is used to space the turnbuckle
catch which is screwed to the block.

THE CAMPER CONVERSION MANUAL

SECTION 10. FITTING THE BED

The following pictures and captions will guide you through the steps involved in this procedure.

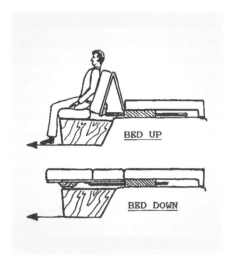

3-10-1. On T3 models, the height of the bed is determined by the height of the engine bay at the rear. Fortunately, this provides a perfect height for the seat when the bed is in the up position.

3-10-3. On T3 models, a bed box is first manoeuvred into place.

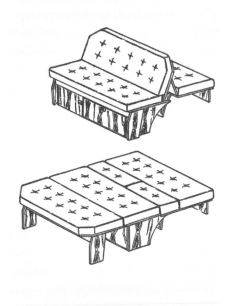

3-10-2. On T4 models, the bed needs to have a separate structure beneath it, and there are different formats available depending on the model you choose. This type provides storage room behind the seat when it's in the up position.

3-10-4. The bed box fits up against the engine housing. Note that on our vehicle, the blown air outlet for the Propex heater has already been fitted to the box before it is installed in the vehicle. Access for cutting the necessary holes would otherwise have been difficult.
The seat box must be screwed to the floor once the correct position has been established. See Pic 19 for the way in which fixing screws are screwed to the floor on the door-side of the seat box and to the kitchen unit on the opposite side.

3-10-5. Roy screws the hinged lid and fixed section of top to the bed box, holding the lid with just a couple of screws to establish its position.

3-10-6. When the position of the lid and fixed section are correct, the remainder of the screws are fitted.

3-10-7. The bed base, complete with its folding mechanism, is now manoeuvred into position in the van.

3-10-8. On T3 models the process is the same, though there's less to manhandle.

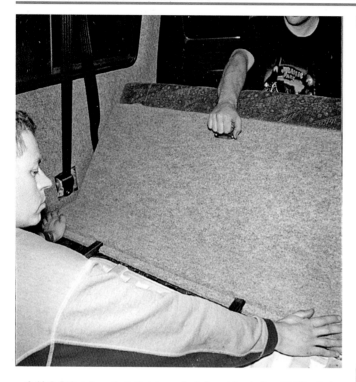

3-10-9. Before it can be bolted down, the Leisuredrive design of folding bed must be raised into the seating position.

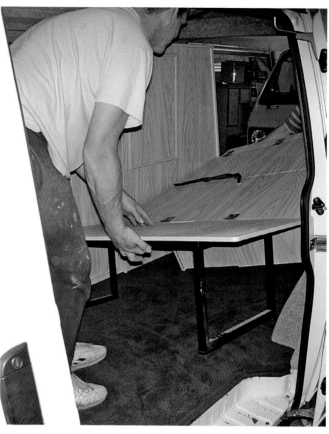

3-10-10. This is the equivalent unit being installed into the rear of a T4.

3-10-11. Once again, the bed has to be placed in the up position before it can be permanently fitted.

3-10-12. The bed base must now be accurately aligned. Here, the folding mechanism is lined up with the ribs on the van floor and the position of the seat is correctly established.

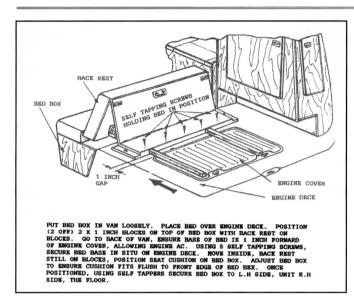

PUT BED BOX IN VAN LOOSELY. PLACE BED OVER ENGINE DECK. POSITION (2 OFF) 2 X 1 INCH BLOCKS ON TOP OF BED BOX WITH BACK REST ON BLOCKS. GO TO BACK OF VAN, ENSURE BASE OF BED IS 1 INCH FORWARD OF ENGINE COVER, ALLOWING ENGINE AC. USING 5 SELF TAPPING SCREWS, SECURE BED BASE IN SITU ON ENGINE DECK. MOVE INSIDE, BACK REST STILL ON BLOCKS, POSITION SEAT CUSHION ON BED BOX. ADJUST BED BOX TO ENSURE CUSHION FITS FLUSH TO FRONT EDGE OF BED BEX. ONCE POSITIONED, USING SELF TAPPERS SECURE BED BOX TO L.H SIDE, UNIT R.H SIDE, THE FLOOR.

3-10-13. The location of the seat base on the bed box at the front and the 1in. (25mm) gap between the engine bay cover and the rear of the bed base are enough to establish the correct position of the bed.

3-10-15. When the relevant holes are drilled, a set of bolts can be used to bolt the unit to the floor.

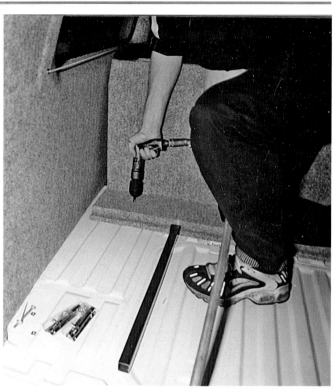

3-10-14. Take extreme care when drilling through the floor to make sure that you don't drill into any of the vehicle components beneath.

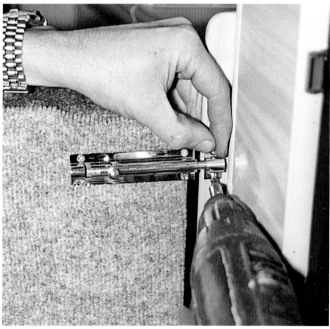

3-10-16. Leisuredrive uses ordinary catches, such as this one, to hold the seat back in the upright position.

3-10-17. On the left-side of the vehicle, the hollow steel section beneath the window has to be drilled to take the bolt on the catch.

3-10-18. The loose cushions can now be fitted in place.

SECTION 11. FITTING THE TABLE SUPPORT
The following pictures and captions will guide you through the steps involved in this procedure.

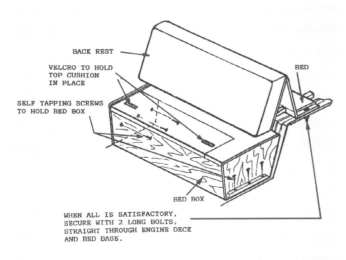

BACK REST

VELCRO TO HOLD
TOP CUSHION
IN PLACE

SELF TAPPING SCREWS
TO HOLD BED BOX

BED

BED BOX

WHEN ALL IS SATISFACTORY,
SECURE WITH 2 LONG BOLTS,
STRAIGHT THROUGH ENGINE DECK
AND BED BASE.

3-10-19. Seat cushions will need to be held with Velcro strips on the seat box. The seat box itself will already have been screwed to the floor in the positions shown.

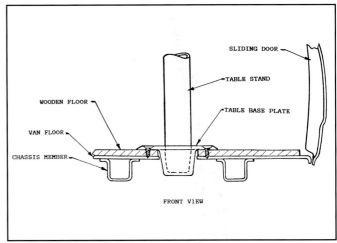

SLIDING DOOR

TABLE STAND

WOODEN FLOOR

TABLE BASE PLATE

VAN FLOOR

CHASSIS MEMBER

FRONT VIEW

3-11-1. Note that the table base plate - shown here on a T3 - must be fitted so as to avoid any obstructions.

3-11-2. Paul uses a tank cutter to cut the required hole size.

3-11-3. Floorboard and van floor edges are protected with primer paint.

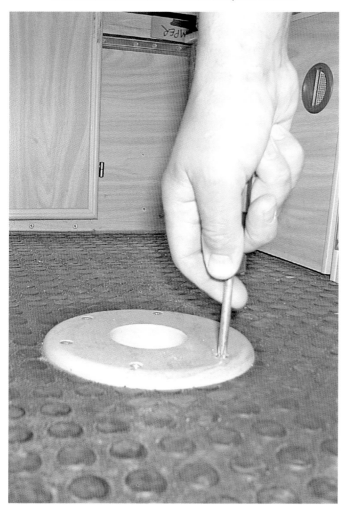

3-11-4. After screwing the table base plate in position ...

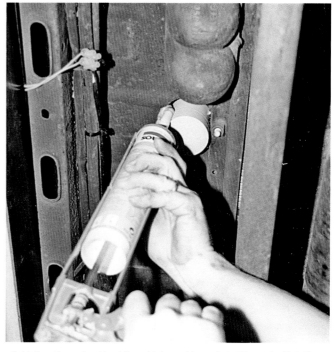

3-11-5. ... the underside of the vehicle must be sealed with mastic. Note those air reservoirs fitted to Syncro T3 models - examples of what to look out for when drilling through the floor.

Chapter 4

Gas, water & electricity

• It's essential that the installation of gas fittings and appliances are only carried out by a qualified professional - a CORGI registered LPG fitter, in the UK.
• It's equally essential that all electrical wiring, appliances and equipment are installed by a qualified electrician - typically NICEIC qualified in the UK. Even 12 volt wiring can cause a fire or gas explosion if incorrectly installed.
• We strongly recommend that you have the relevant work carried out by qualified professionals. However, there is no reason why you shouldn't carry out the preparatory work yourself. For instance, you could fit the electrical power unit to the side-wall and run the wiring in position (though leaving it accessible so that it can be professionally checked). Similarly, gas appliances, such as cooker or water heater and pipe runs, can be fitted into position but not connected.
• Have all connections made by appropriately qualified professionals. Pay to have a thorough check carried out, and certified that the installation is complete and safe, ready to present to your insurance company.
• From 2003 in the UK, appliances and regulators fitted to all new caravans and motor caravans, operate at a different gas pressure to that of all older appliances.

Do not mix-and-match appliances and/or regulators from the different eras!

This is the most safety-critical chapter of this manual. That's not to say that you shouldn't carry out any of the work yourself, but you will certainly need to bring in the professionals to carry out final installation and checking of safety-critical areas. I can do no better than to quote from the web site of The Self-Build Motor Caravan Club www.sbmcc.fslife.co.uk on the subject of safety. "Safety should never be compromised for the sake of speed, money, or apathy. If personal safety is not enough to make people 'do things right' what about insurance claims ... ? Insurance companies may be perfectly within their rights to not honour a claim when something like badly installed wiring leads to a fire. Even if it [the wiring] is not the cause of the fire, the claims assessor could, and will use, it as a reason not to pay!"

LPG regulations
All caravans and campers built after 1 September 2003 have to conform to the EU standard known as EN1949, which specifies that the regulator will be a fixed part of the gas supply. Therefore, in place of the potentially dangerous piece of push-on rubber hose with a hose-clip, is a pipe with fitted ends from the fixed regulator to gas bottle. Push on hoses are no longer

allowed under the new regulations. All new hoses must have threaded connectors, and must have excess-flow and non-return safety valves.

The advice for self-build installers in the UK is simple: You should strongly consider using the EN1949 standard for the following reasons: the system is standard in the UK and in Continental Europe, and it will, therefore, be much more convenient to use; all new appliances are designed to run at the new, higher pressure, so the regulators must match the requirements of the appliances being fitted; it's safer.

Standard EN1949
LPG gas installation standard EN1949 came into effect in September 2003 for National Caravan Council certified caravans and motor homes.
• At present, users require a regulator for each type of gas they use: 28mbar for

One of the special, bulkhead-mounted regulators which are installed in new caravans and motorhomes. (Courtesy Calor)

butane and 37mbar for propane.
• All models built after August 2003 must be fitted with an EN 12864, Annex D, 30mbar regulator by the manufacturer. (In most cases this will be fitted to the gas bottle locker wall.)
• The new regulator is designed to be able to supply propane or butane, both at 30mbar (the European standard).
• Three new hoses - now known as pigtails - are available in the UK:

1. Calor-type 4.5 kg butane cylinders with a hexagonal fixing nut.
2. Calor-type 3.9kg & 6kg propane cylinders.
3. Campingaz cylinders with an M20 x M20 adapter.

Which gas?
If you plan to spend a lot of time in Continental Europe, you may want to stick with Campingaz. Cylinders are widely available on both sides of the Channel, and there will be no need to have a different pigtail for each country. For Campingaz, an M20 x M20 hose connection is required, plus a Campingaz adapter.

If you choose not to use the (often more expensive) Campingaz, you will need to obtain a pigtail connector to match the cylinders available in the country you are visiting. The new connector is used to replace the UK pigtail (attached to the bulkhead regulator), while you're using the European cylinder, and then switched back when back in the UK.

Can the system be retro-fitted?
Most motorcaravans built in the last 10 years will have appliances manufactured to comply with the Gas Appliance Directive, and will be designed for an operating pressure of 30mbar. **It is essential that you check the appliance data plate, instructions, or contact the appliance manufacturer or local dealer. If you are not sure, don't have the later system retro-fitted!**

Maintenance
Gas appliances must be installed in accordance with the safety requirements of British Standards and EU regulations, or other local laws. All gas appliances must be serviced annually to keep them in a safe and efficient condition. The service must be carried out by a qualified engineer and should include:
• Check gas cylinder storage, which should be in an area insulated from the interior of the motorcaravan.

• Ventilation check. Air inlets and cylinder storage ventilation should be clear and adequate.
• Gas leak check, condition of pipework and hoses and compatibility of fittings.
• Flue check: Smoke spillage test.
• Appliance safety devices must work correctly.
• Appliances must be safe for further use.

ORDER OF WORKING
There can be no hard and fast rules about which bits to fit first and which to leave until last. But there will certainly be some jobs that are best carried out before the furniture is fitted, some that can only be carried out after it's fitted, and some, no matter how hard you try, that you'll wish you'd done before fitting something else in place! One important point relates to the fitting of gas and electrical components mentioned at some length in the rest of the introduction to this chapter. You may wish to route pipes and cables so that they can be seen (from inside cupboards of course - not across the interior of the 'van!) so that the professionals who check, connect and certificate gas and electrical installations can see exactly what's there and where it all goes.

Don't forget, of course, that there's nothing to stop you fitting furniture then taking it out again later if you need to. For that reason, it's sometimes best to use round-head coach-bolts and nuts rather than screws. Screws will only go into wood a limited number of times before their grip weakens and they become useless. If you're using chipboard screws, you

should not expect to be able to remove and replace them once fitted. All of the furniture shown here has been constructed from laminated material screwed to 25mm x 25mm battens, or screwed-and-glued where no dismantling can possibly be necessary in future. In a few cases, such as the bed box mountings to the structure of the van, I have replaced fixing screws with nuts and bolts. It's surprising how many times that bed box has had to come out so that the components inside it could be maintained!

You should also bear in mind the possible need to access components such as a Belling Malaga water heater. The heater was originally built into the units on our van. The heater was fitted and the sink unit fitted over it. Then, when it needed maintenance, there was the threat of having to remove the whole sink unit. I cut out a panel from the sink unit and refitted it with a neat trim strip to cover the join, but how much better it would have been if an access panel had been built in from the first. Hindsight is a wonderful thing - but forward planning is the next best ...

SECTION 1. WATER PUMP AND PIPEWORK
Give some thought to where the water pump will go at the design stage. It's not something that will need to be accessed on a regular basis, but when you need to get at it, you don't want to have to dismantle furniture. The pump is a mechanical object and prone to failure, and it may need servicing from time to time. Bear in mind the following important points:

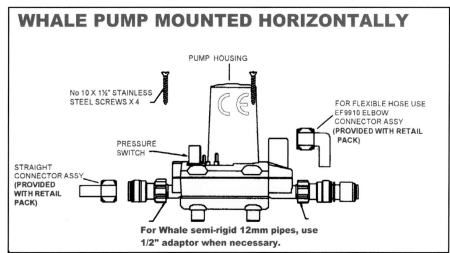

WHALE PUMP MOUNTED HORIZONTALLY

PUMP HOUSING

No 10 X 1½" STAINLESS STEEL SCREWS X 4

FOR FLEXIBLE HOSE USE EF9910 ELBOW CONNECTOR ASSY (PROVIDED WITH RETAIL PACK)

PRESSURE SWITCH

STRAIGHT CONNECTOR ASSY (PROVIDED WITH RETAIL PACK)

For Whale semi-rigid 12mm pipes, use 1/2" adaptor when necessary.

4-1-1. These are the components of the Whale Clearstream 700 kit and show the alternative pipe fittings for use with different locations and different types of pipe.

• Don't fit the pump on the outside of the vehicle where it may be damaged by water or debris thrown up by the wheels.
• It's best to mount the pump in a relatively well-insulated area, such as inside a cupboard, and not fixed directly to the exterior of the van to reduce risk of frost damage.
• You must take note of the manufacturer's instructions on the correct orientation of the pump. For instance, the Whale Clearstream 700 pump shown being fitted here can be mounted either horizontally or vertically (although Whale recommends mounting the pump horizontally for best results), but must not be mounted upside down.
• Leave room for a water filter between pump and tap if you want to fit one.

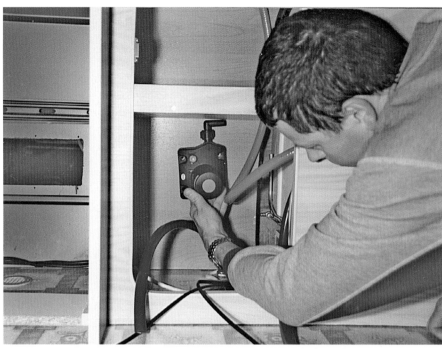

4-1-2. The approximate positions of the pipe runs have already been established, and the location of the Whale pump is now being sorted out. It has to be far enough away from shelves and other fittings so that the pipes can be fitted to it, but it is best towards the top of the cupboard area so that heavy objects placed on the floor of the cupboard won't knock against it.

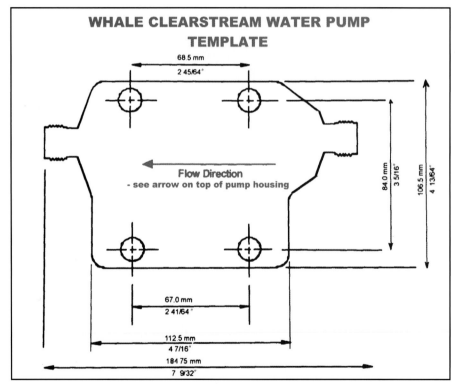

WHALE CLEARSTREAM WATER PUMP TEMPLATE

68.5 mm
2 45/64"

Flow Direction
- see arrow on top of pump housing

84.0 mm
3 5/16"

106.5 mm
4 13/64"

67.0 mm
2 41/64"

112.5 mm
4 7/16"

184.75 mm
7 9/32"

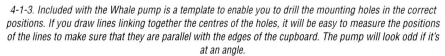

4-1-3. Included with the Whale pump is a template to enable you to drill the mounting holes in the correct positions. If you draw lines linking together the centres of the holes, it will be easy to measure the positions of the lines to make sure that they are parallel with the edges of the cupboard. The pump will look odd if it's at an angle.

4-1-4. Before it can be fitted into the vehicle, the correct pipe adaptors need to be fitted to the pump.

4-1-5. It's a good idea to cut to length the pipes which go to the taps, and to fit them to the pump while it's out of the cupboard.

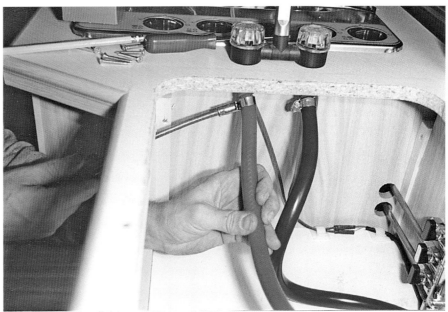

4-1-6. The pipes to the taps can then be fed into position and clamped to the pipe fitting on the base of each tap. Note that it's far easier to carry out this work with the sink not yet fitted to the sink unit.
Note also that the wiring from the taps has not been connected but has been clipped into place ready for connection later.

FITTING THE PUMP

• Mark the four hole positions shown on the template and drill holes for screws using a 4mm ($^5/_{32}$in) drill.
• Make sure that the pump is fitted with the water flow in the correct direction as indicated by the arrow on the top of the pump housing.
• Screw the pump into place but do not overtighten the screws because otherwise the anti-vibration buffers on the base of the pump will not be able to sufficiently absorb the vibration in the pump.

PREPARING THE WATER SYSTEM FOR WINTER

• If you don't drain the water system frost can cause severe damage to the pump, taps and water heater, if fitted.
• Drain the water tank. If your water tank has no drain tap fitted to it, open all the taps and allow the pump to pump the tank dry.
• Disconnect the hose to allow it to drain out at the lowest point in the system. You may have to disconnect more than one hose to do this.
• Remove the outlet hose on the pump, turn the pump on and pump out any remaining water. **Don't** let the pump continue to run once it's empty.
• Reattach the hoses now so that you don't forget them next season.

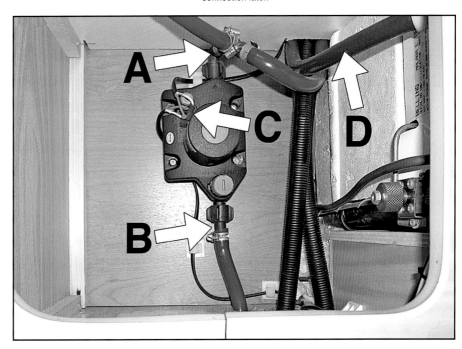

4-1-7. Note that in this instance, with a hot-and-cold connection, the outlet to the pump (A) has to go off in two directions - one to the cold tap and one to the hot water heater. The inlet (B) comes from the storage tank. The feed to the hot tap (D) comes from the hot water heater, when fitted.
The wiring (C) giving a power feed and a switch operated from the taps is connected in accordance with the wiring instructions that come with the pump.

SECTION 2. WATER STORAGE
TANK

In this section we show how to fit an under-floor water storage tank. The tank we used is from a company called CAK Tanks which manufactures a huge range of plastic tanks so that you'll be able to find one suitable for just about any installation. We also show the fitting of a Zig tank level gauge.

4-2-1. The Zig level gauge is fitted to the front of the wardrobe unit, just beneath the place where the Zig main power unit will go later. This is the sort of component that is most easily fitted before the furniture is installed in the vehicle. You can also connect tags of wires onto the back with bullet or spade connectors on their ends, ready to be connected when the furniture is in place.

4-2-2. The CAK plastic water storage tank needs to be drilled accurately so that the water level gauge can be fitted.

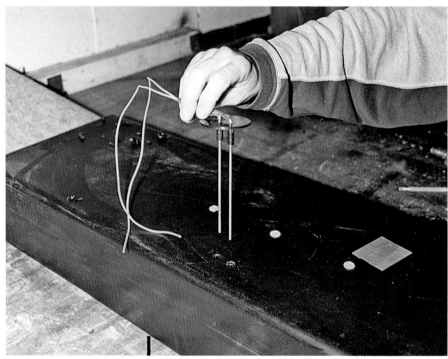

4-2-3. Make sure that the level gauge you buy is the correct one for the tank; it's best to do as we did and purchase it from the supplier - in our case CAK Tanks - to ensure that they match.

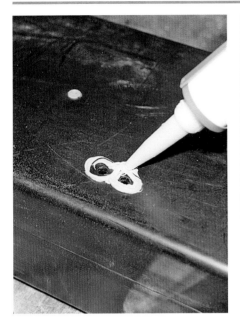

4-2-4. Use silicone sealant around the seating of the level unit so that it can't leak.

4-2-5. Once the tank has been fitted to the underside of the vehicle, access will inevitably be more difficult. For this reason, Leisuredrive fitted to the tank a short length of hose with a connector in it ...

4-2-6. ... and also connected the drain tap to the tank before it was fitted to the vehicle.

4-2-7. Mounting the tank to the underside of the vehicle is achieved using the brackets and threaded rods provided with the CAK tank. Inevitably, some ingenuity and careful thought will be needed. This tank was purchased to fit between two chassis rails, which made it relatively easy to find locations for the hooks holding the clamps in place.

4-2-8. The tank is best first fitted in a dummy run to work out the precise locations for the clamps.

SAFETY FIRST!
• Wear goggles! It's far safer than closing your eyes and hoping for the best!

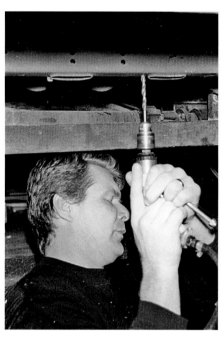

4-2-9. When clamp positions been established, any holes can be drilled in the chassis. Bare metal holes should be treated with paint or wax preservative to prevent them from rusting.

4-2-10. Leisuredrive made up a timber support panel to go underneath the bottom of the tank which was slipped into place along with the tank when it was offered up beneath the vehicle.

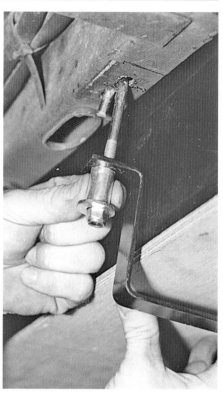

4-2-11. The threaded clamp bars were hooked into place and lengths of tubing used as spacers to establish the correct length so that the tank clamps could be pulled up nice and tight - but not too tight because you don't want to damage the plastic tank!

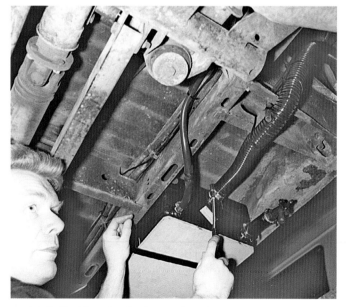

4-2-12. The inlet and outlet pipes can finally be fitted to the tank and their clamps fully tightened when the tank is in place.

4-2-13. This then enables you to run the water pipe into convenient positions underneath the vehicle, making sure that it is clipped or cable tied in a non-vulnerable position.

4-2-14. You will need a tank cutter to cut the bodywork in the location you choose for the tank filler.

4-2-15. This is the tank filler cap assembly ready to be fitted to the newly-cut hole.

4-2-16. The hole has to be de-burred with a file ...

4-2-17. ... before it's painted to prevent it from rusting.

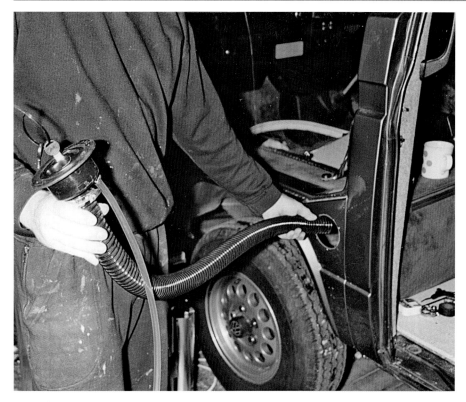

4-2-18. The tank hose can now be introduced into the hole in the bodywork and the tank filler assembly pushed into place.

4-2-19. This particular filler cap was held in place with three stainless steel screws. The screws were fitted after drilling suitable size pilot holes in the body.

4-2-20. It won't have escaped your attention that the water filling point is not completely dissimilar to a fuel filler. Make certain that the water filler is correctly labelled with the legend DRINKING WATER ONLY, because this isn't a cocktail that you will ever want to mix!

SECTION 3. ELECTRICS

When a new house is built, you don't put in the cooker, the light fittings and the wall sockets before the wiring. You put the cables in first, having established where all the electrical components are going to go, and leave enough spare wire to connect them later. In this instance, the analogy with a motor caravan is a good one because you'll first need to establish where everything is going to go, run the wiring in place while the structure of the motor caravan is being built, and leave enough spare wire at each end to make the connections when the electrical components are fitted.

Do bear in mind the point made at the start of this chapter with regard to electrical safety, and the need for having your electrician check the safe location and security of electrical cables when they are in place. For that reason, you may wish to run cables inside cupboards where they can still be seen by the electrician who will be checking the job over. In the instance shown here, the qualified personnel at Leisuredrive ran cables behind wall and roof coverings before they were fitted into place. If you decide to run cables inside cupboards, you may wish to purchase plastic channelling from a DIY store. This comes with a clip-on cover so it can easily be accessed for checking or for adding more cables later, but then the cover can be fitted to tidy the job and make the cabling secure.

SAFETY FIRST!

• Each electrical component will need to have the correct grade of cable.
• **Do not** under any circumstances use mains electricity cable for 12 volt wiring. Its characteristics are completely different and it can readily overheat and catch fire on a 12 volt system.
• Find out from the instruction book with each appliance the rating of cable that will be needed and, if it isn't clear, contact the manufacturer or have the electrician who will be carrying out the check advise on the grade of cable to be used.
• Suitable 12 volt cable is manufactured by companies such as Ring (see the suppliers list in the back of this book), and can be purchased from most automotive DIY stores.

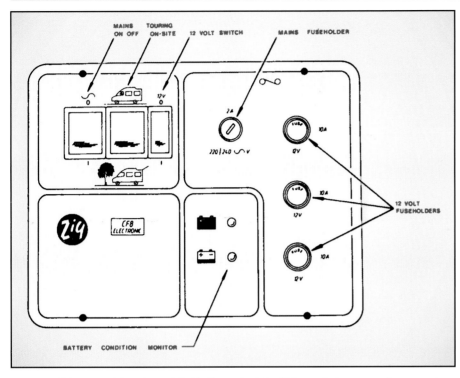

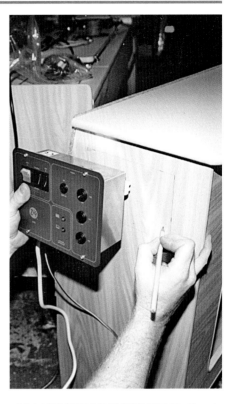

4-3-1. This is one of the units made by Zig Electronics Ltd. which manufactures a very fine range of electricity units for all types of caravan and motor caravan. This is the CF8 battery charging and distribution system and includes the following features:
• Automatic battery charging control for charging the leisure battery when the engine is running.
• Mains battery charging up to 12 amps, depending on battery state.
• Mains-to-12 volt conversion up to 4.5 amps continuous current.
• Switchable selection of power source.
• Double pole mains switch - useful in mainland Europe where positive and negative feeds are frequently interchangeable because double pole switches are the norm there.
• Six protection devices to eliminate overheating.

4-3-2. YOU CAN DO THIS YOURSELF: The Zig unit is fitted to the wardrobe before the wardrobe is fitted to the vehicle. Zig recommends that the inside of the cupboard to which the unit is fitted must allow a free space of at least 25mm all the way around the unit, and that includes a space from the back of the unit to any cover that may be fitted. One of the reasons is that the unit may get hot in normal use.

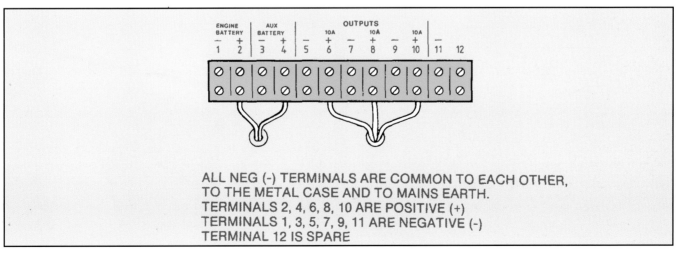

4-3-3. YOU SHOULD NOT DO THE FOLLOWING ELECTRICAL JOBS YOURSELF: Unless you are a qualified electrician that is. These are some of the connections at the terminals on the CF8 unit.

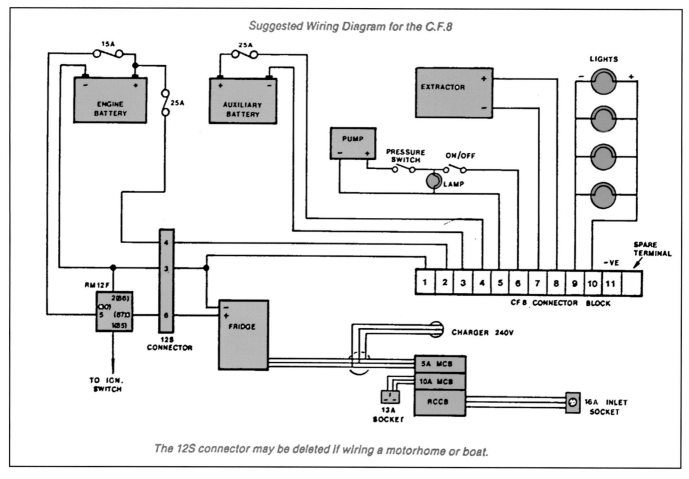

Suggested Wiring Diagram for the C.F.8

The 12S connector may be deleted if wiring a motorhome or boat.

4-3-4. This wiring diagram illustrates the way in which the CF8 unit must be wired into the battery, charging circuit and power supply circuits by your auto-electrician.

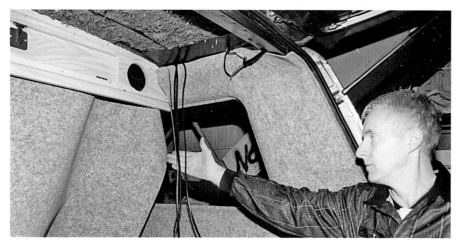

4-3-5. If you are able to follow the basic principles of the wiring diagram, you may be able to run the wiring into place as you build the interior of the motor caravan, but bear in mind what was said earlier in this section with regard to making the cables accessible.

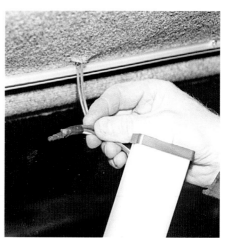

4-3-6. The idea will be to leave ends of cable ready for your electrician to connect up the relevant components.

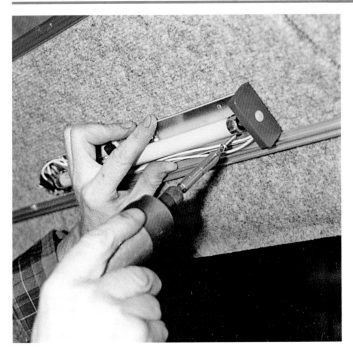

4-3-7. There's no reason why the components themselves should not be fitted in place and, in fact, your electrician would probably welcome this because it would save him a certain amount of preparatory time and enable him to get straight on with the wiring.

4-3-8. This is the 240 volt wiring being connected behind the driver's seat to:
- Mains supply on-off double-pole switch.
- Consumer unit with safety cut-out devices.
- Twin 13 amp sockets.

4-3-9. There will be a number of 12 volt connections required at the front end of the vehicle, in close proximity to the vehicle battery and/or leisure battery. Your electrician will also need to add a relay, such as the Zig RM14, which controls the supply of 12 volt power to the fridge and ensures that the fridge is only receiving 12 volt power when the engine is running, and so prevents the battery from being drained.

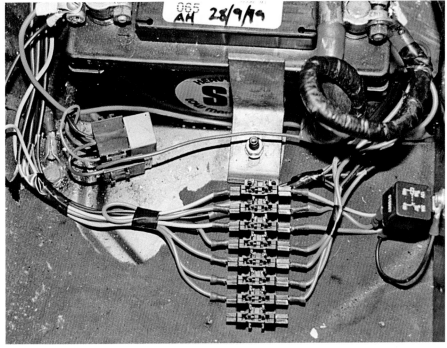

4-3-10. The areas beneath the seats are particularly useful for making such connections, and it's a good idea to have any fuse blocks or connection blocks fitted to the wiring ...

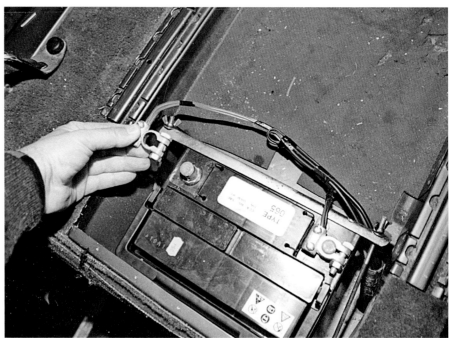

4-3-12. The last connection to be made will be the feed and earth wires to the main battery and leisure battery, for the obvious reason that you don't want power going around the circuit until your electrician is on site to check that everything is okay.

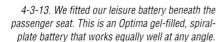

4-3-11. ... before screwing them down. Don't leave them loose because it would then be possible for them to move around and possibly short out against some of the vehicle's bodywork.

SAFETY FIRST!
• Make absolutely certain that the battery won't touch the surrounding metalwork.
• A normal height battery will short out on the seat base which can cause a fire.

4-3-13. We fitted our leisure battery beneath the passenger seat. This is an Optima gel-filled, spiral-plate battery that works equally well at any angle.

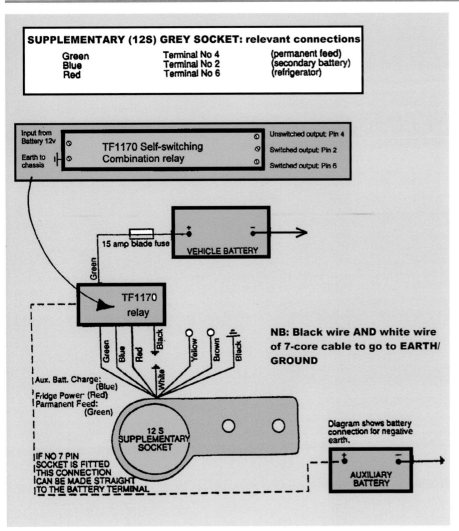

SUPPLEMENTARY (12S) GREY SOCKET: relevant connections

Green	Terminal No 4	(permanent feed)
Blue	Terminal No 2	(secondary battery)
Red	Terminal No 6	(refrigerator)

Input from Battery 12v

Earth to chassis

TF1170 Self-switching Combination relay

Unswitched output: Pin 4
Switched output: Pin 2
Switched output: Pin 6

15 amp blade fuse

VEHICLE BATTERY

TF1170 relay

Green | Blue | Red | Black | Yellow | Brown | Black | White

NB: Black wire AND white wire of 7-core cable to go to EARTH/ GROUND

Aux. Batt. Charge: (Blue)
Fridge Power (Red)
Parmanent Feed: (Green)

12 S SUPPLEMENTARY SOCKET

Diagram shows battery connection for negative earth.

IF NO 7 PIN SOCKET IS FITTED THIS CONNECTION CAN BE MADE STRAIGHT TO THE BATTERY TERMINAL

AUXILIARY BATTERY

4-3-14. There's no reason why you shouldn't tow a trailer or even a suitable caravan behind your camper conversion. If you do so, you will need to fit a supplementary 12S socket to supply power to a caravan with another set of special connections and relay. Again, for safety's sake, this is a job for an auto-electrician. The equipment itself can be purchased from Ryder Towing Equipment - see the suppliers list in the back of this book.

4-3-15. While the wiring was being connected to our motor caravan, I couldn't resist having one small extra that is simple for an electrician to fit and extremely useful. Here, a hole is being drilled in the wardrobe at the rear of the camper.

4-3-16. A cigarette lighter socket purchased from an auto-accessory store can now be installed to give you a source of power at the rear of the camper for a mobile phone, lap-top or 12 volt cool box when you go on a shopping trip.

THE CAMPER CONVERSION MANUAL

SECTION 4. REFRIGERATOR

Fitting the refrigerator yourself brings together all three assembly elements: DIY, professional electrician and professional gas fitter work. There's a certain amount of construction work involved in fitting the fridge to the furniture, in making it draught-proof and in making it secure. While it's a good idea to run the gas pipework and electrical wiring into position, you will need to have professionals make the actual connections, as discussed at the start of this chapter.

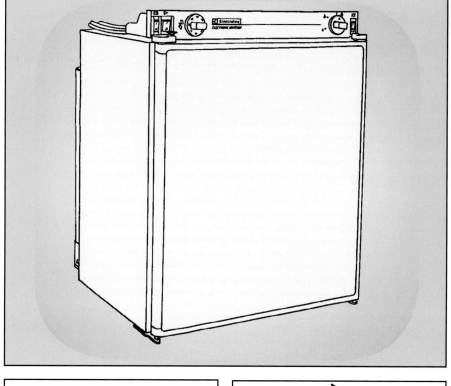

4-4-1. Dometic fridges - formally known as Electrolux - are the doyenne of caravan and motor caravan fridges and have a proven track record of quality and service backup. There's a whole range of fridge sizes available, although obviously you would be hard pushed to fit one of the larger ones into a small motor caravan of this type!

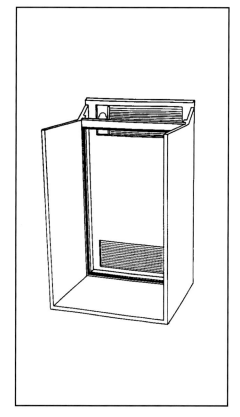

4-4-2. This is illustrative of the kind of structure into which the Dometic fridge should be fitted. The sides and the top will need to be sealed between the fridge and the interior of the motor caravan. The rear of the fridge must have open access to a pair of vents, one at the top and one at the bottom.

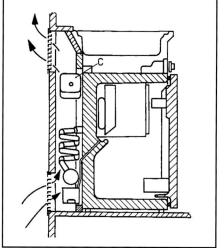

4-4-3. This is so that cool air can be drawn in through the bottom vent at the rear of the fridge and pass over the heating element on the back of the fridge, before being expelled by convection through the vent towards the top of the fridge. If the fridge is not sealed between its sides, top and base, and the inside of the motor caravan, the essential air which is used to pass over the elements on the rear of the fridge and allow it to work will create a draught inside the vehicle.

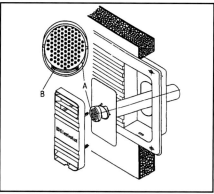

4-4-4. When the fridge is working on LPG (gas) combustion takes place and carbon monoxide, among other gases, is produced. The exhaust from the combustion process would be potentially toxic were it not for the fact that the exhaust is vented directly out of the motor caravan as shown here. This part of the installation is also something that will have to be checked by your qualified gas fitter. It will have to be disconnected in order to gain access to the rear of the fridge when he connects the gas pipes, so he will also check the connection of the exhaust when he refits the fridge to the vehicle. Preparing the vents, and the exhaust through the walls of the motor caravan, is another part of the work that you may be able to carry out yourself.

4-4-6. On the opposite side of the fridge door to the hinges is the latch which is used to hold the fridge door shut when you are on the move, and to hold it fractionally open when the fridge is not in use. It is essential that this is done because otherwise the interior of the fridge will go mouldy and smell horrible.

4-4-5. Jumping ahead a little here, but one of the simpler jobs you can do for yourself is to decide which side the door hinges will hang on. They are easily interchangeable and we fitted ours so that the fridge door opened with the opening towards the living room.

4-4-7. Here the electrical connections are being made to the back of the fridge with suitable lengths of cable to allow the main loom to be connected to the fridge once it's in place. If you don't leave this part of the work to a qualified electrician you must have him check it with the fridge out of its location.

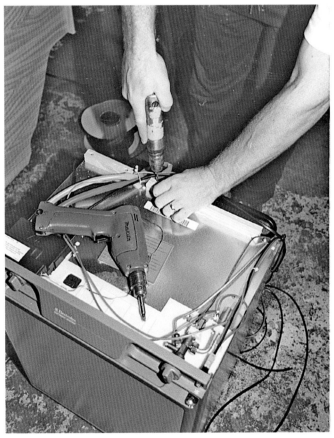

4-4-8. A batten is being screwed to the top of the fridge at the very back where there is no danger of screwing into the interior of the fridge.

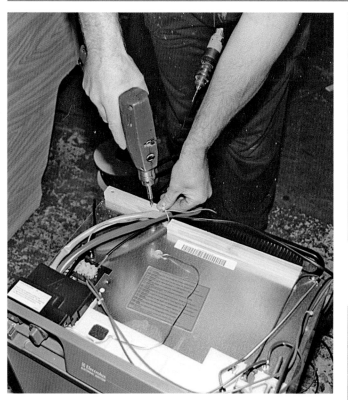

4-4-9. This batten is then used to screw down cable clips as appropriate, and also for part of the air baffle, as will be shown later.

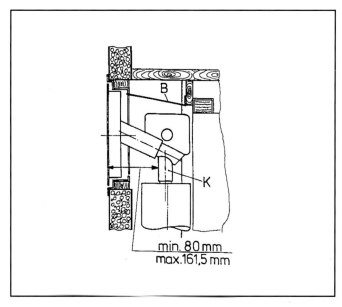

4-4-11. The rear of the fridge must not be pushed against the rear of its enclosure. As this Dometic/Electrolux drawing shows, there must be a gap of at least 110mm between the back of the fridge and its enclosure and the top vent must be suitably located at the height shown.

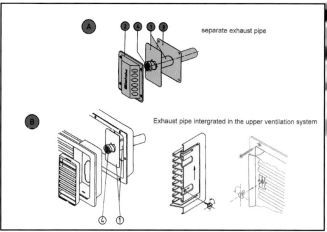

4-4-10. Dometic/Electrolux uses one of two types of exhaust system. One of them (A) has a separate exhaust outlet. The other (B) has an exhaust integrated with the upper vent.

4-4-12. The pipe provided for the exhaust has to be cut to length. Unless, like Leisuredrive, you are fitting lots of these units, it would be best to leave this cutting until the fridge position has been finally established.

4-4-13. The air deflector is fitted to the top of the fridge and is screwed to the batten shown earlier.

4-4-14. When it's time to fit the fridge - and bear in mind that this part of the work must only be carried out by qualified personnel - the baffle, cables and gas pipework have to be carefully eased into position.

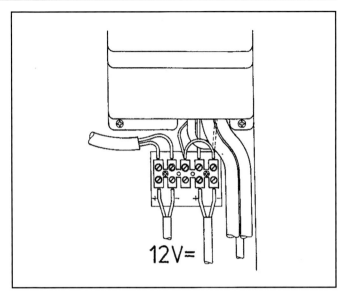

4-4-15. Your electrician will be able to use this diagram to connect the main supply cable, which is the right-hand cable in this drawing. When an auto-ignitor is fitted, a separate supply cable can be connected to a constant, fused 12 volt supply.

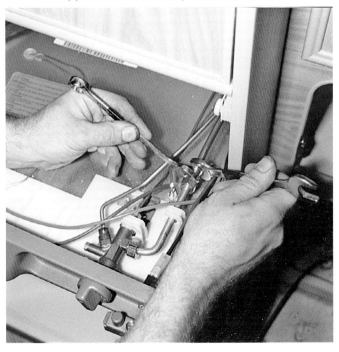

4-4-16. A qualified gas fitter can now make the gas connections.

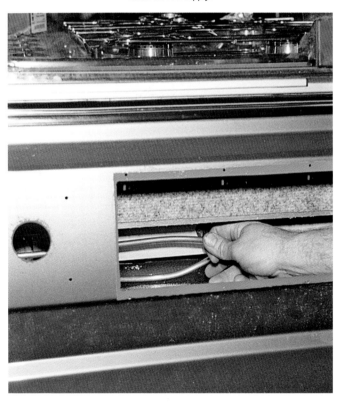

4-4-17. When the fridge is pushed fully into position, the gas connections to the main wiring supply can be made through the vent hole in the side of the vehicle's bodywork.

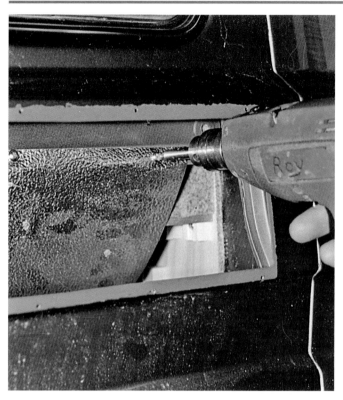

4-4-18. The same access hole can be used to screw the vent baffle to the interior of the vehicle's bodywork. Don't forget to seal down the sides of the baffle.

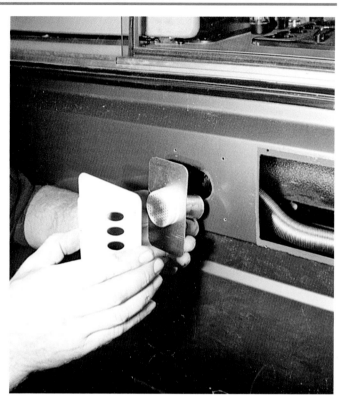

4-4-19. The exhaust outlet is fitted to the vehicle side in a similar fashion.

4-4-20. The vents are simply screwed to the bodywork - best to use stainless steel screws to prevent corrosion - and the rear surfaces of the vents must be carefully sealed with silicone to prevent any ingress of water.

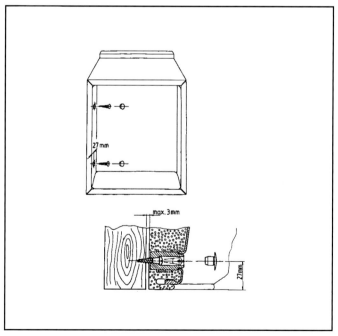

4-4-21. Holes are provided in the sides of the fridge to enable you to screw the fridge firmly to the furniture surround. Lever out the plug (bottom) ...

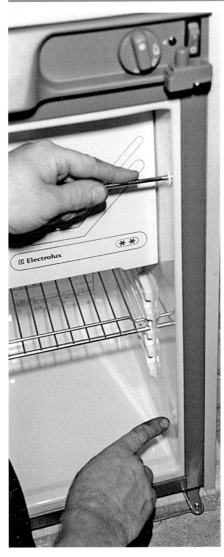

4-4-22. ... before screwing the fridge into place and refitting the plugs.

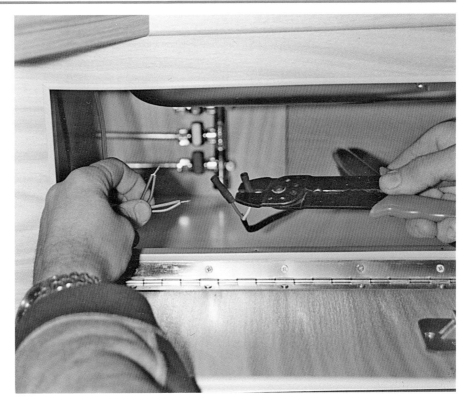

4-4-23. The lengths of cable connected to the fridge should have been fed through into the cupboard space as the fridge was pushed into place so that the feed connections can now be made by your electrician.

SECTION 5. COOKER AND SINK

Spinflo supplied both the cooker and the sink shown in this section. Both were purchased from the same source so that they have a complementary appearance. And it works - they look good together!

The cooker will, of course, need a qualified gas technician to connect it and an electrician will need to complete the wiring to the sink taps which are, after all, simply switches to turn on the pump. However, once again there is a large amount of work involved in installing the components, even if the final connections have to be made by the specialists.

4-5-1. As you will have seen in an earlier section, the furniture will have been pre-cut to take the cooker hob and sink.
- It's best to trial-fit both cooker and sink before the unit is placed in the motor caravan but then to remove them before lifting the unit in.
- It saves weight, removes the risk of causing damage and provides you with the access you will need to screw the furniture in place and install other surrounding components such as fridge and water heater.

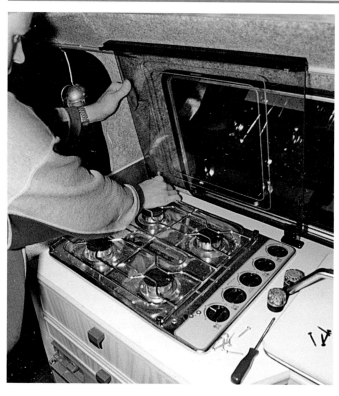

4-5-2. On our motor caravan, a glass lid was fitted, also from Spinflo, to give a complementary look to the hob unit.
- This is an essential feature because it provides a splash panel when you are cooking and an extra work surface when you're not.
- The glass top is simply screwed to the back of the cooker unit and is best located after the unit has been fitted into the motor caravan so you can make sure the top fits without fouling any of the surrounding furniture or bodywork.

4-5-3. In this particular installation - a T4 Transporter - a separate hinged splash panel is being fitted to the end of the cooker unit. In many ways this is a preferable idea because it allows the driver's seat a little more rearward movement - the headrest can catch on a fixed splash panel - which is invaluable for those with longer legs.

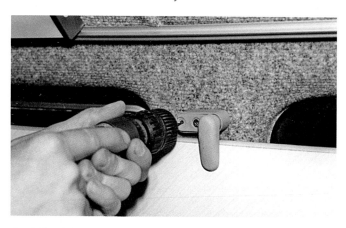

4-5-4. The sink unit also has a hinged cover and it's necessary to fit a clip to one of the pillars between the rear windows to hold the cover up when the sink unit is being used.
- The Spinflo cover over the cooker is spring-loaded and holds itself in the up position.

4-5-5. The Spinflo cooker hob is in, the taps are in place, the sink cover is fitted, but the sink has not yet been put in place. This provides access to clip the gas pipes and taps for the cooker and fridge to the rear of the sink unit. The taps obviously need to be easily accessible.

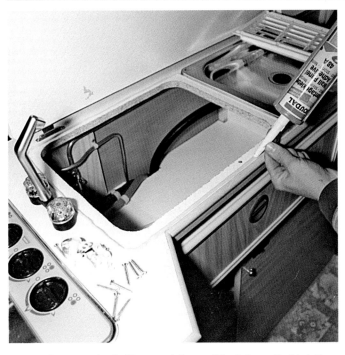

4-5-6. Silicone sealant had been used all around the drainer unit - this is the matching Spinflo drainer with built-in drain plug - and now sealer is being applied to the sink unit top.

4-5-7. The unit is lowered in place evenly on the sealer. If you lower first one side and then the other the sealer may be pushed out of position on the side you lower first.

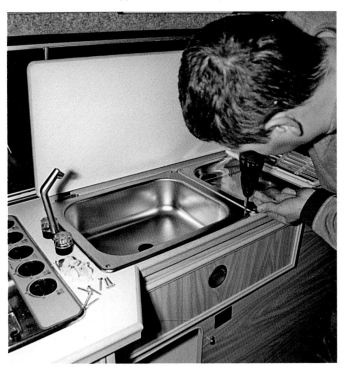

4-5-8. The sink can be screwed down and any excess sealer wiped off as it squeezes out from underneath the sink.

4-5-9. It then remains to fit the drain to the bottom of the sink, again using sealer to make sure that there is no leak into the cupboard beneath. Note how the gas taps are easily accessible from beneath the sink bowl. If they had been fitted any higher, they wouldn't have been!

4-5-10. The two drain pipes are run through the cupboard and out through holes in the bottom of the motor caravan floor.

SECTION 6. PROPEX BLOWN AIR HEATER

The Propex blown air heater is a gas-operated heater with a 12 volt fan. This enables you to heat the interior of the motor caravan even when on a site without mains electricity. It's efficient and it's thermostatically controlled and, although the blower is a touch noisy, it's a lot better than being cold. We have used in on winter picnic trips as well as on cool evenings when camping.

4-5-11. It then only remains to fit the burners and the cooker top, plus the grill pan components, if fitted, for the installation of the Spinflo units to be completed, all but for the professional gas and electrical connections on the cooker and taps respectively.

When siting the heater underneath the seat box, you have to bear in mind that there has to be an unrestricted air inlet to the heater casing. Soft items placed inside the seat box can easily block the inlets on the heater casing. I constructed a steel case to go around the heater casing, open at both ends and with an air gap of about 25mm all around the heater so that the ingress of air is far more difficult to block off.

SAFETY FIRST!

• There are both LPG (gas) and electrical connections on the Propex Heat Source 1600 and these will need to be fitted by qualified personnel in the usual way.
• The Propex heater also has safety requirements with regard to the exhaust of the burned gases from the combustion process. The exhaust must be suitably located away from fuel lines, electrical cables or anything flammable, either inside or beneath the vehicle. It must also be away from the entry door and away from any position where combustion products may enter the interior of the vehicle.
• If you intend installing the Propex heater yourself (prior to having qualified personnel connect it up), consult a qualified gas

engineer with regard to the siting of the heater unit and the location of the hole to be drilled in the floor for positioning the exhaust. Propex strongly recommends that the exhaust pipe outlet vents beyond the outer edge of the vehicle floor, not beneath it.

4-6-1. The outlet vent for the Propex heater needs to be fitted near to the floor, and preferably near the door so that it is heating cooled air and keeping the interior of the motor caravan as warm as possible. As with so many other small fitments, it was easier to cut the hole for this vent and to fit the vent cap before the bed box was fitted to the vehicle.

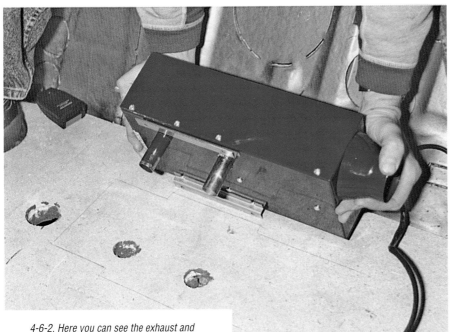

4-6-2. Here you can see the exhaust and combustion air holes, plus the larger air vent hole to the left of them, drilled in the floor of the vehicle. It's obviously important that you check the underside of the vehicle with very great care to ensure that you're not going to be drilling through chassis members, electrical, brake, fuel, or any other components when drilling these essential holes in the floor.

4-6-3. The combustion air pipe and the longer exhaust pipe are both pushed onto the spigots.

SAFETY FIRST!
• Route the exhaust so that it discharges beyond the side of the vehicle.
• There must be no possibility of lethal exhaust gases seeping upwards into the vehicle.

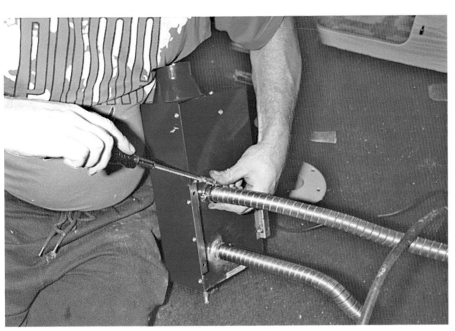

4-6-4. They are then fixed in place with jubilee clips. The bracket on the bottom of the Propex heater raises it sufficiently off the floor to enable these jubilee clips to be fitted.

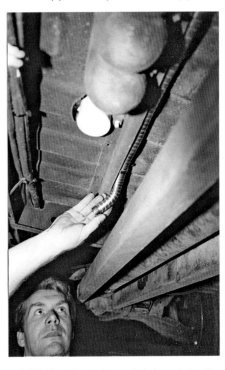

4-6-5. The exhaust pipe needs to be routed well away from the hole in the floor through which it came, and well away from any other vent holes in the floor, and should face the rear of the vehicle so that no water or debris is forced into the pipe as the vehicle is driven.

4-6-6. Bending and shaping the gas pipes before clipping them to the vehicle's bodywork is something that you can do yourself.

4-6-7. Making the gas connections to the heat source must only be carried out by a qualified gas fitter. You can now see the 'drop' vent to the left of the heat source which is a necessary requirement for any gas-operated equipment housed in the vehicle.

4-6-8. Once the bed box has been fitted to the vehicle, it's possible to connect the blower pipe to the vent on the bed box and to the heat source itself.

4-6-9. The thermostat is best located in an open space at about half-way up the height of the interior of the vehicle. In our case, the best space available was on the side of the wardrobe, as shown here. Make sure that the thermostat is not mounted in direct sunlight or above a cooker or fridge.

Wiring Instructions.

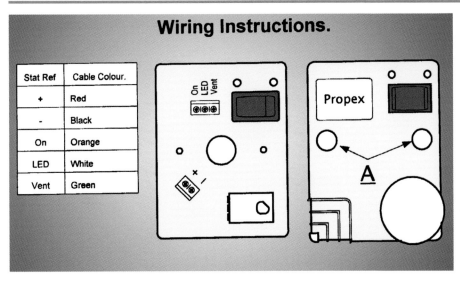

Stat Ref	Cable Colour.
+	Red
-	Black
On	Orange
LED	White
Vent	Green

4-6-10. Your electrician will need to connect up the thermostat, as well as the wiring to the heat source itself, using the colour scheme shown here.

4-6-11. The thermostat with cover in place fitted to the wardrobe side.

FACT FILE: FITTING NOTES

1. The size of the holes for the exhaust spigots are 30mm and need to be cut with a tank cutter.

2. The hole size for the hot air outlet and recirculation air inlet vent need to be cut to a diameter of 95mm.

3. Propex recommends that the exhaust outlet should protrude a short way beyond the edge of the vehicle.

4. The combustion air pipe should terminate at least 0.5 metres away from the end of the exhaust.

5. Both pipes should have a slight downward slope to prevent any possibility of water traps.

6. The wiring to the thermostat and Heat Source 1600 is supplied with the kit and consists of two wiring looms with terminals and housings to plug into the main printed circuit board inside the heater.

SECTION 7. WATER HEATER

The Maxol Malaga E water heater is pretty well a standard fitting in good quality caravans and motor homes, although it's not often fitted to smaller motor caravans. The identical looking Malaga heats and stores hot water using gas only, whereas the Malaga E can be used from mains electricity, gas or a combination of both for very rapid water heating.

See Section 1. Water pump and

pipework for information on draining the water heater to prevent winter frost damage.

SAFETY FIRST!

• As with so many other of the appliances shown here, installation of the gas and electrical systems are jobs for qualified personnel only.

• See manufacturer's data for installation requirements - Malaga GE 13.5 litre model shown in illustration 7-31.

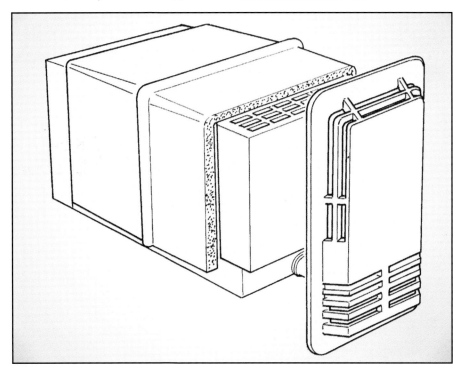

4-7-1. The Malaga and Malaga E come as complete kits of parts ready to be fitted to the vehicle. The inlet and exhaust pipes are built in to the unit and are covered by the external vent plate shown here.

4-7-2. You have a chicken-and-egg situation when it comes to working out the correct location of the heater. You'll need the cupboard to be in place to see where the heater will fit properly, but you'll need the cupboard out again in order to be able to fit the heater.

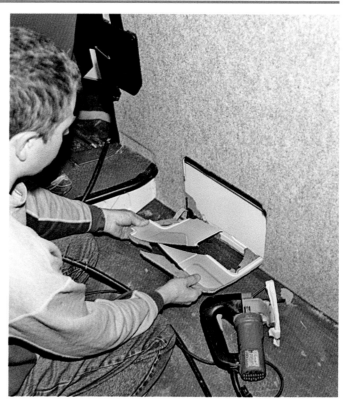

4-7-3. If the interior wall coverings have all been fitted before the heater is installed, you have to cut them away before deciding on the final location of the heater. Bearing in mind that the exhaust and inlet pipes are fixed, you will need to get the position of the heater right first time in relation to the outside wall of the vehicle.

4-7-4. Just to one side of the Malaga E, fit a low level vent to enable heavier-than-air gases to drop out of the enclosed space in which the heater will be situated.

4-7-5. Once the holes are drilled they should be painted to protect both the bare steel through which you will have drilled and the edges of the floorboard. IMPORTANT NOTE: Before drilling any holes do make sure that there are no chassis rails beneath that part of the floor and - even more importantly - that there are no fuel, brake, electrical or other components beneath the area through which you will drill.

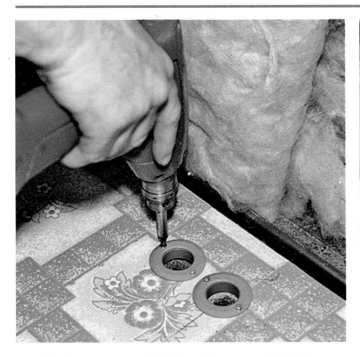

4-7-6. The drop vents consist of plates which are screwed to the floor ...

4-7-7. ... followed by plastic grilles which prevent the entry of uninvited furry visitors.

4-7-8. In this location, Steve works out the position of the Malaga heater, bearing in mind how far the exhaust will protrude through the sidewall. If there is any floor covering in the area where the water heater will stand you must remove it to a width of 320mm, 450mm-inward from the motor caravan wall.

4-7-9. On a T3 Transporter, the curvature at the bottom of the van side means that you will need to make a box to raise the heater towards the more horizontal part of the van sidewall.
The height of the box will depend on the amount of headroom you have in the cupboard. Note the way in which the vent fits to one side of the box; it must not be obscured by it.

4-7-10. Ensure, by measuring and checking, that the position of the heater won't clash with anything fitted to the outside of the van. When you are certain of this, you can mark the position of the heater on the sidewall.

4-7-11. Using a small bit, drill through the top corner of each mark, the two holes corresponding with the two top corners of the Malaga heater.

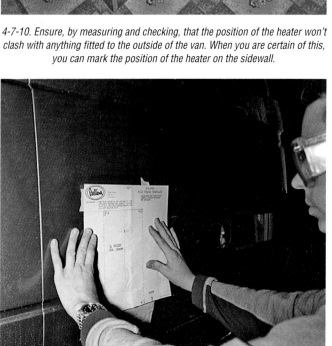

4-7-12. On the outside of the van, Steve uses the template provided with the kit and lines it up with the two holes he has drilled in the bodywork. The template is held onto the body with small pieces of masking tape, and a further two holes are drilled to mark the bottom two corner positions.

4-7-13. Several layers of masking tape are used to fulfil two purposes at once. One purpose is to mark the exact position of the cutting lines when cutting out for the Malaga heater. Having placed several layers of broad masking tape in position, each of the four holes is enlarged so that each hole is big enough to take a jigsaw blade.

4-7-14. The jigsaw is then used to cut out the exact shape required. Now you can see the second of the two uses of the strips of masking tape. The shoe of the jigsaw would normally mark paint quite badly, usually necessitating a respray.
By placing several layers of masking tape over the bodywork and another couple of layers of masking tape on the bottom of the jigsaw shoe, you won't mark the paint and will save yourself a lot of extra work and expense putting right paint faults.

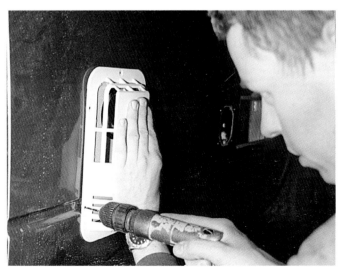

4-7-16. The next step is to screw the flue cover to the outside of the motor caravan wall. It must be precisely centrally placed over the hole you have cut.

4-7-15. It always makes sense to cut a little way inboard of the shape that you finally want. At this stage you can trial fit the heater making sure that it aligns correctly with the hole and, when you're satisfied that it does, use the file to remove any burrs and paint the edge of the hole to prevent any corrosion.

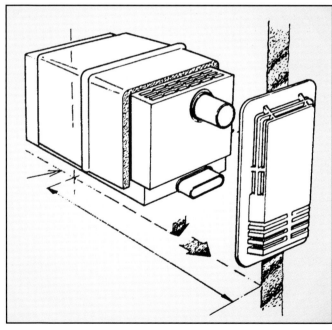

4-7-17. To make sure that the heater is perfectly located, draw a centre line on the floor and another one vertically up the back of the heater casing. Slide the exhaust on the heater through the flue seals on the plate that has just been fitted to the outer wall until it reaches the stop position. Check that both the flue and the air intake pipes pass through the lip seals on the outer vent cover. Line up the vertical mark on the rear of the heater with the centre line on the floor and screw the heater to the floor.

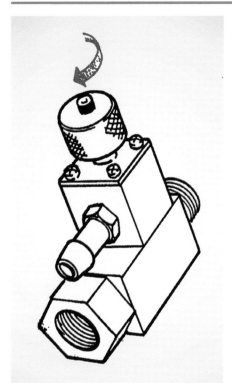

4-7-18. The drain tap will already be fitted to the heater unit - seen with the casing removed - and note that the tap is closed when the knob is turned anti-clockwise, not clockwise as would be the case with most taps.

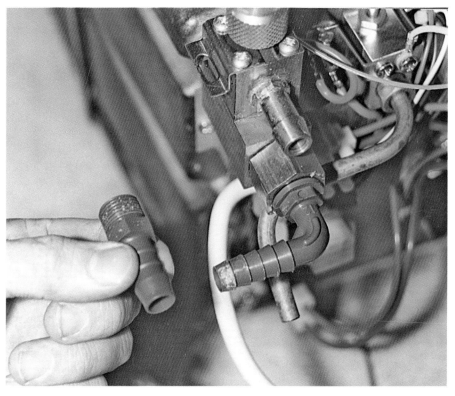

4-7-19. In the case of a Leisuredrive conversion, there isn't enough depth for the standard water outlet (held in left-hand), to be used so an elbow has to be fitted in its place.

4-7-20. You can carry out this part of the work yourself but you should not make the final gas fittings. The gas pipe will have to make some tight bends in order to fit neatly within the cupboard space.

Top tips!
- If the pipe needs to be straightened and rebent, it will work harden.
- In this case, scrap the pipe and use new.
- You may be able to use an automotive brake or fuel pipe bender if you don't have access to the correct plumber's tool.

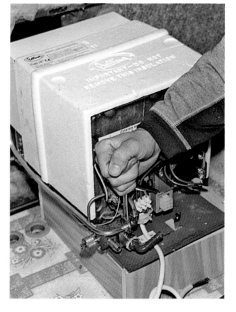

4-7-21. If you do fit the pipe temporarily in place to check its position, don't tighten the union or the olive will be squashed onto the pipe. Leave that to the professional fitter.

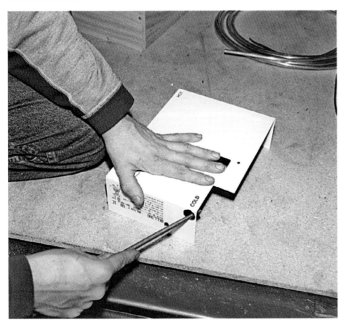

4-7-22. With the pipe in place and taken in this particular direction, it was necessary to open out and, in one place, to cut away part of the casing.

4-7-23. The casing is simply screwed onto the back of the unit.

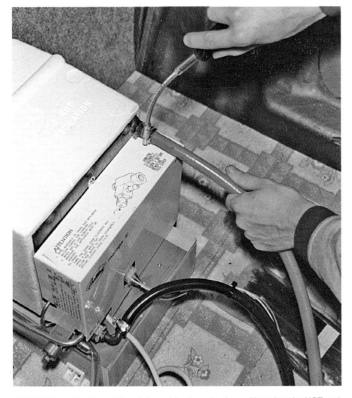

4-7-24. You should use ½in reinforced food quality hose. Note that the HOT and COLD connections are clearly marked and it's essential that they are connected correctly.

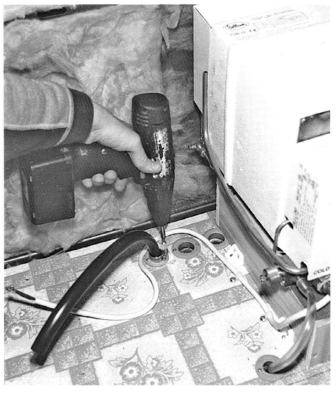

4-7-25. The electrical cable, not to be fully connected unless you are a qualified electrician, can be held in place with cable clips.

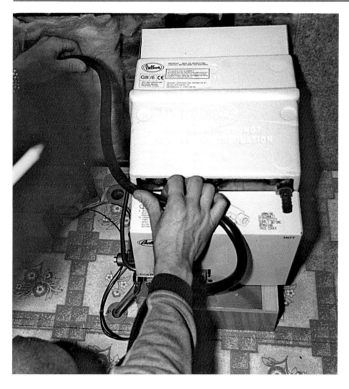

4-7-26. The water pipe should also be clipped neatly in place.

4-7-27. In the case of a T3 Transporter, the wooden box on which the heater is sited will need to be screwed to the floor.

4-7-28. The operating switch panel can be fitted to a convenient part of the kitchen unit.

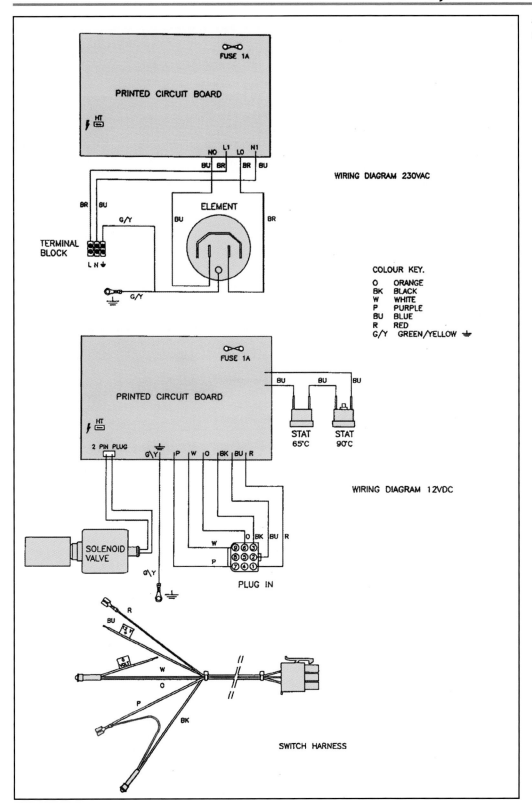

4-7-29. The wiring comes with its own looms ready to be plugged in.

FUSE 1A

PRINTED CIRCUIT BOARD

HT

NO L1 LO N1

BU BR BR BU

WIRING DIAGRAM 230VAC

BR BU

G/Y

ELEMENT

BU BR

TERMINAL BLOCK

L N

G/Y

COLOUR KEY.

O ORANGE
BK BLACK
W WHITE
P PURPLE
BU BLUE
R RED
G/Y GREEN/YELLOW

FUSE 1A

PRINTED CIRCUIT BOARD

HT

BU BU BU

STAT 65°C

STAT 90°C

2 PIN PLUG

G\Y P W O BK BU R

WIRING DIAGRAM 12VDC

O BK BU R

SOLENOID VALVE

W

P

G\Y

PLUG IN

R

BU

W

O

P

BK

SWITCH HARNESS

4-7-30. The final step for someone electrically qualified, such as Leisuredrive's Steve, seen here, is to connect up the mains and 12 volt wiring feeds.

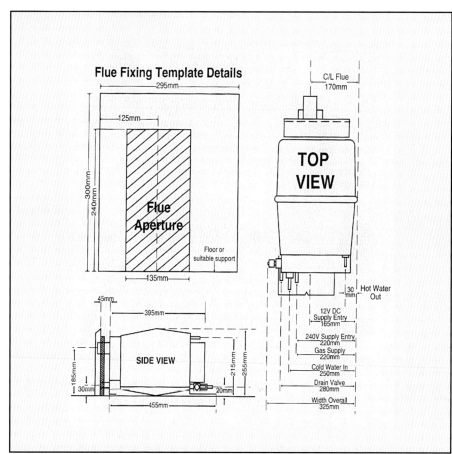

Flue Fixing Template Details

295mm
125mm
300mm
240mm
Flue Aperture
135mm
Floor or suitable support

C/L Flue
170mm

TOP VIEW

30 mm | Hot Water Out

45mm
395mm
185mm
30mm
455mm
SIDE VIEW
20mm
215mm
255mm

12V DC Supply Entry 165mm
240V Supply Entry 220mm
Gas Supply 220mm
Cold Water In 250mm
Drain Valve 280mm
Width Overall 325mm

4-7-31. Installation requirements for the Malaga GE 13.5 litre model: The flue terminal position should not be closer than 300 mm below an opening window or 600 mm from a vertical corner. Clearances required for installation and servicing, as seen from inside the installation:
LHS = 240mm
RHS = 5mm
Rear = 100mm
Top = 5mm

Chapter 5
Interior trim

As far as the seats go, it's unlikely that you'll carry out a great deal of this work yourself, though making your own curtains is something you might want to have a go at. The great majority of converters will use the services of someone such as Leisuredrive's trimmer, Nigel, who carried out the work shown here.

• For bedding, a number of caravan and motor caravan trim specialists advertise in the pages of caravan and motor caravan magazines. They will make up bedding covers and even complete, covered, bedding cushions for you.
• Vehicle seat covers can be made by any vehicle trimmer worth his salt - see your local *Yellow Pages* for those near you.
• You will need to liase with both of them to make sure that the cloth matches and that you're buying the right sort of cloth for both jobs. It's by far best if you can buy all the cloth from one single source, or it probably won't match.
• If you do make up your own bedding, don't be tempted to use cheap foam. You need top quality Dunlopillo-type foam otherwise it will compress and may 'sweat' excessively as you lie on it, and will rapidly disintegrate in use.
• Take your tape measure while looking at seat bases at your local caravan dealer to help you decide on an appropriate

thickness of foam. Discuss your needs with your specialised caravan upholstery supplier.

Van seats are often badly worn, especially if the vehicle has been used for delivery work and, in any case, they're not usually in the sort of 'fun' fabrics that you associate with your holiday home on wheels. Stripping down and reupholstering a van seat is certainly 'do-able' at home, though it's not beginners' stuff. On the other hand, making up new seat covers would require considerable skill and the use of an industrial sewing machine, to cope with the great thicknesses of material - a domestic machine simply wouldn't be up to the job. So, the following section is for instruction if you can buy the seat covers, or for information, if you can't ...

SECTION 1. SEAT REMOVAL AND STRIP DOWN
The following pictures and captions will guide you through the steps involved in this procedure.

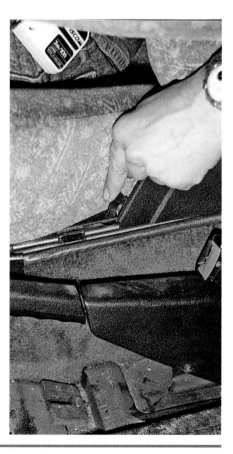

5-1-1. On the T3 Transporter, to remove the seat, slide it forward as far as it will go and then tip back this locking tab at the rear of the seat to allow it to move past its end stop on the runners.

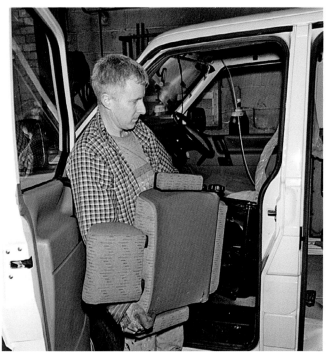

5-1-2. Hold the adjuster catch in the unlocked position, slide the seat right off the runners and lift it out of the vehicle.

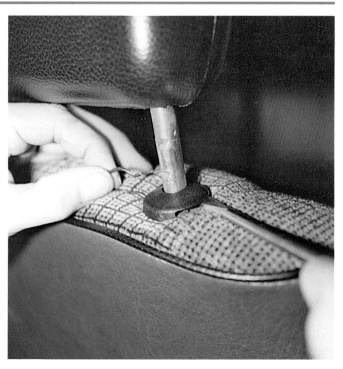

5-1-3. To remove the headrest, push out the 'hair grip' clips from inside the clip retainer and lift away the headrest.

5-1-4. After levering out the finisher button and removing the fixing screw on the most common type of armrest (also see Section 2: Re-covering seats), unscrew the armrest bracket from the side of the seat.

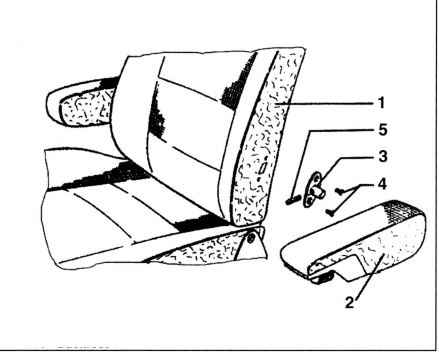

5-1-5. This adjustable type is very similar. 1. backrest, 2. adjustable armrest, 3. mounting pin, 4. countersunk screw, 5. dowel pin.

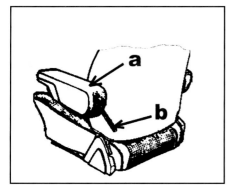

5-1-6. Press the cover of the armrest (a) as far as possible away from the seat until the dowel pin can be seen.
Drive out the dowel pin with a drift (b).
Pull the adjustable armrest off the mounting pin.

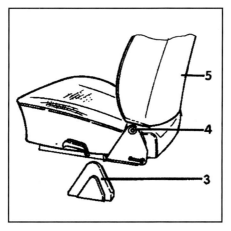

5-1-7. A plastic trim cover (3) unclips from the seat hinge (4).

5-1-8. Lever the cover off and lift away.

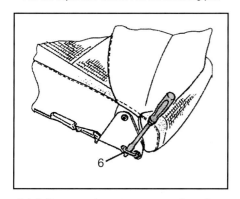

5-1-9. To remove the seat runners, you first release the spring (6) with a lever ...

5-1-10. ... then remove the spring from the seat runner release shaft.

5-1-11. The runners can then be unscrewed from the seat frame.

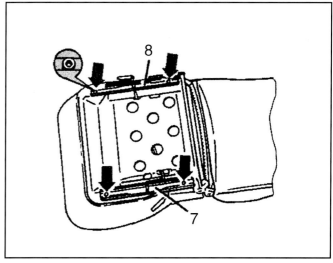

5-1-12. These are the four socket-head screws (arrowed). After removing the right-hand runner (7), remove the left-hand runner (8).

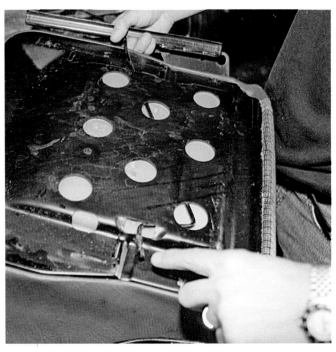

5-1-13. From one side of the seat, the right-hand seat runner, complete with release mechanism, is drawn out of its location on the seat.

5-1-14. To separate the seat back, you take out the retaining screw from one side.

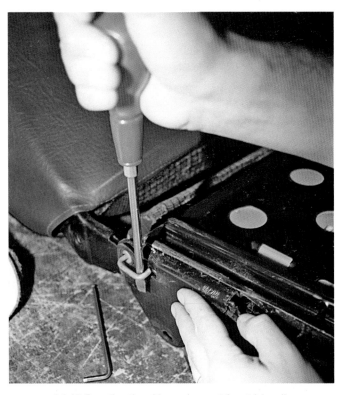

5-1-15. From the other side, you lever out the retaining clip.

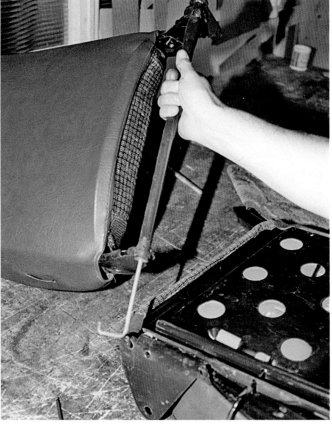

5-1-16. Slide the clip free and remove the seat back from the seat base.

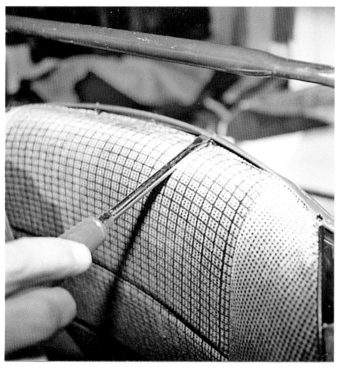

5-1-17. The rear panel on the seat back is held at its base with steel clips - normally concealed when the seat is assembled. Lever up the clips.

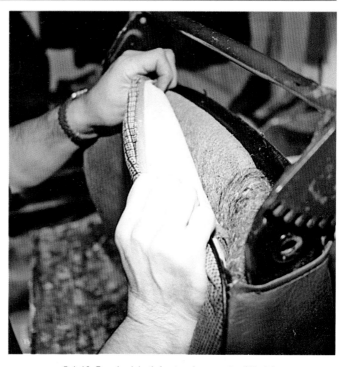

5-1-18. Ease back both front and rear parts of the trim.

5-1-19. Remove any wiring holding part of the trim in place.

5-1-20. Stiff wires pass through the ends of both the front and rear panels and these can be slid out.

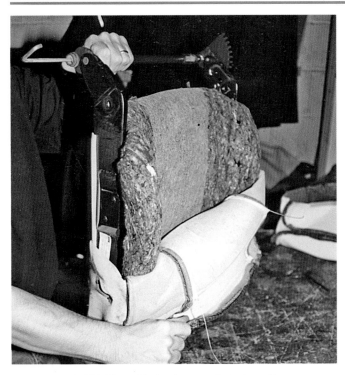

5-1-21. The seat backrest can now be 'undressed.'

5-1-22. To remove the headrest inserts, you may need to twist them to free them from the seat frame.

5-1-23. The headrest inserts and seat covers can now be taken away as one.

5-1-24. The seat base pushes into a recess around the perimeter of the underside of the base.

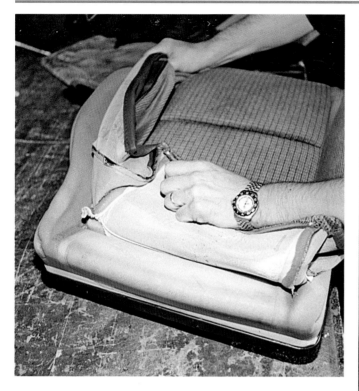

5-1-25. The base material can now be lifted away all around the seat.

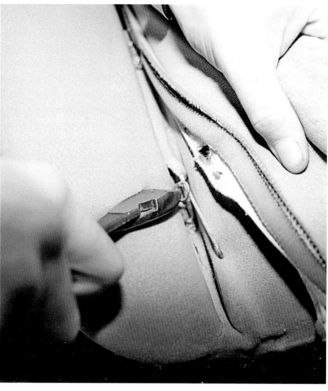

5-1-26. The seat's 'shape' is held down into the rubber via these hog rings which have to be cut away with side cutters.

SECTION 2. RE-COVERING SEATS

The following pictures and captions will guide you through the steps involved in this procedure.

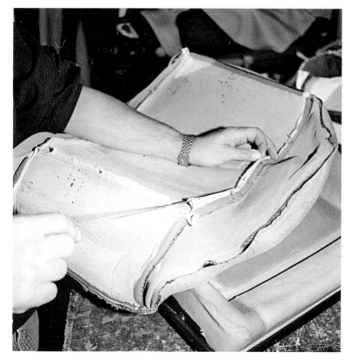

5-1-27. The stiff wires onto which the hog rings were clipped can be pulled out of the seat base cover once it has been removed from the base.

5-2-1. Nigel makes up the seat trims using the same fabric that has been used for the bed base and rear seat backrest.

5-2-2. He slides on the new backrest cover, making sure that it fits evenly both at the top and all down the seams along the sides.

5-2-3. The seams at the bottom of both front and rear panels now have to receive their retaining rods.

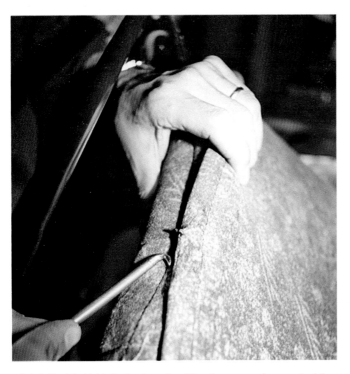

5-2-4. Nigel first folds the front panel and then the rear panel over each of the sharp clips in turn.

5-2-5. Each clip is then tapped back down flat with a hammer.

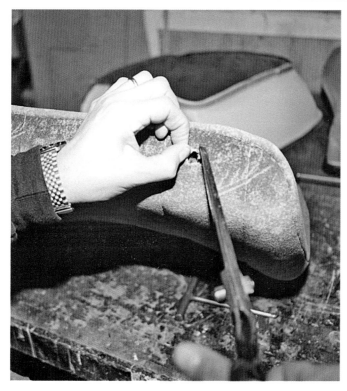

5-2-6. In the top of the backrest, a small piece of cloth is cut where each of the headrest supports is fitted.

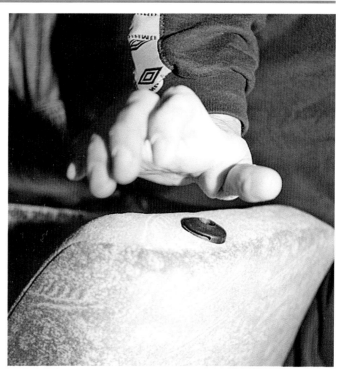

5-2-7. Each headrest support is then clipped firmly into place.

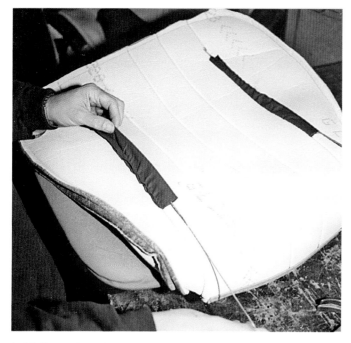

5-2-8. The seat base trims are turned inside out and the seam along the inside of each one receives its fixing rod.

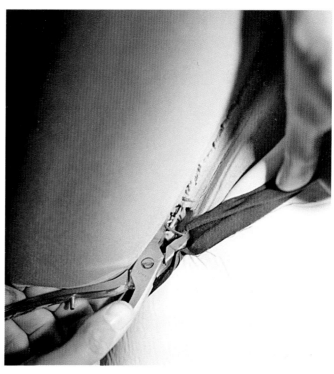

5-2-9. Each rod is held down to the seat base using new hog rings. Nigel uses professional hog ring pliers for the job.

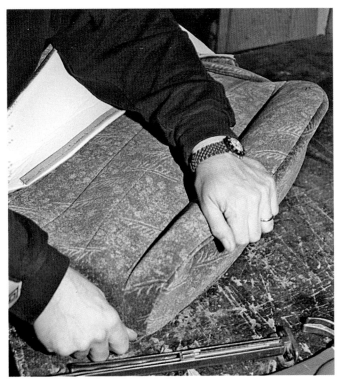

5-2-10. The seat base cover is pulled evenly and firmly over the edge of
the seat.

5-2-11. The flap of material is folded into the retaining channel ...

5-2-12. ... and pushed firmly in with a screwdriver, making sure that the material
is sufficiently tensioned to remove any wrinkles that might otherwise be found
in the cloth.

5-2-13. The seat runner channels and adjuster bar are refitted as the reverse of
the process shown in Section 1.

5-2-14. The hinge rod, extended fully from the tube on the back of the seatrest, is located in the plate on the end of the seat back.

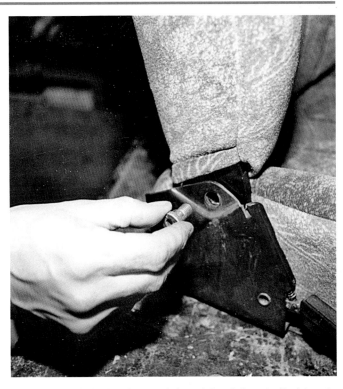

5-2-15. When the backrest is correctly located, the clip is pushed back in and, on the other side, the retaining screw refitted, as shown here.

5-2-16. After marking the positions carefully with a pen, small incisions are made in the side of the backrest. These are to allow the armrest bracket retaining screws to pass through into the captive nuts beneath.

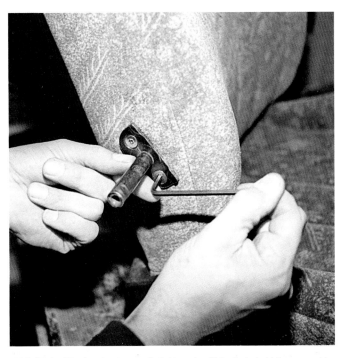

5-2-17. An Allen key-head screw is tightened sufficiently to hold the armrest in place while leaving just enough friction to prevent it from flopping about.

5-2-18. Finally, the trim finisher is pushed into the armrest, folding excess fabric down behind it and concealing the screw head.

SECTION 3. BED BASES AND CURTAINS

The following pictures and captions will guide you through the steps involved in this procedure.

5-2-19. Nigel shows off yet another pair of elegantly re-trimmed Transporter seats.

5-3-1. As we mentioned at the start of this chapter, you will need to make sure that the bed base materials match - or at least complement - those used on the front seats. Leisuredrive uses top quality bedding foam, and Nigel, the trimmer, makes up the finished mattresses. The rear one is shown here being slid into place.

5-3-2. The backrest part of the rear seat forms the centre of the rear bed and is a fixture in the vehicle, being hinged down when the bed is lowered, but the seat base is removable and is held in place with two Velcro strips.

5-3-3. If you want curtains, you have to have curtain track. Leisuredrive uses aluminium curtain track and its position is carefully established so that the fixing screws go into the hollow box section above the line of all of the windows.

5-3-4. Take the curtain track and mark the position of each bend that will be needed.

5-3-5. Aluminium curtain track can be bent into a gentle curve but if you bend it too far and put a kink in it, the runners will jam. It pays to try them out before fitting them to the vehicle.

Top tip!
• If you use plastic curtain track, run the section of track that you will be bending under the hot tap until it becomes hot and flexible, bend it carefully into shape and hold it there while it cools.

5-3-6. For the sake of privacy, the curtain track over the front screen will need to be bent so that one side overlaps the other. The most convenient way of doing this is to bend it around the mirror mounting point on vehicles where the mirror mounting is situated here.

5-3-7. When the positions of the runners have been established, extra holes can be drilled and more screws added to support the flexible track all along its length.

5-3-8. Carefully work out where you want the curtain ties to go. These are necessary to prevent curtains from closing themselves as you drive - a potentially dangerous hazard. The curtain ties are screwed to the hollow box section in a similar way to how the curtain runners have been fitted.

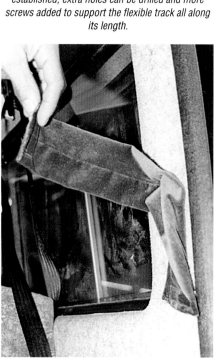

5-3-9. A matching curtain tie with a strip of Velcro at each end is screwed to the sliding door pillar.

5-3-10. The curtains are fitted to the track in the same way as domestic curtains.

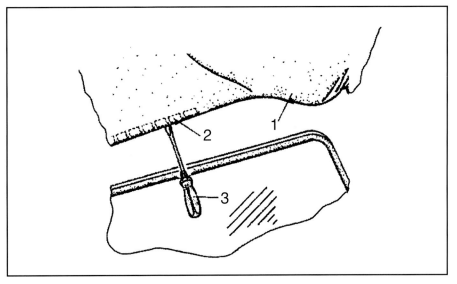

5-4-1. To remove the old headlining:
* *Using a wide screwdriver (3), bend open the serrated strip (2).*
* *Detach the headlining (1) from serrated strip (2).*
* *Pull headlining attachment rods out of their mounting sockets and take them out with headlining.*

5-3-11. This is the ideal location for the rear window curtain tie because it holds the curtain well clear of the rear window.

SECTION 4. CAB HEADLINING

The following pictures and captions will guide you through the steps involved in this procedure.

T4 headlining

For details of the T4's headlining see Chapter 3, Section 1.

T3 headlining

The following pictures and captions will guide you through the steps involved in this procedure.

5-4-2. Leisuredrive makes up new cab headlining to match that in the rest of the camper. The first job is to cut excess material from the seams that run from side-to-side across the headlining. Refer to the old headlining to see how far this cut needs to go. The old headlining will have been removed by springing in the sides and removing the rods as shown in this section.

5-4-3. Each of the rods, retrieved from the old headlining, is pushed into the seams in the new headlining.

5-4-4. To refit, in outline:
* Insert the headlining attachment rods (2) in their mounting sockets (3).
* Align headlining (1) with attachment rods (2).
* Insert the edge reinforcement (5) into the serrated strip (4).
* Use a plastic hammer to bend over the serrated strip (4).

5-4-5. The headlining rods are positioned in the roof channels in the same places they came from. The trim is removed from around the door, the edges of the headlining glued down, the surplus cut off and the door trims pushed back into place.

5-4-6. At the front, the headlining is glued to the top rail in the same way.

5-4-7. The mounting positions for the rear view mirror are found by feeling through the headlining and the fabric cut away.

5-4-8. Mountings for the sun visors, including those for the side clips, are also 'found' by feeling, and then cut out as necessary.

Chapter 6
Extras & accessories

This chapter is about those little extras that can make all the difference. The list of potential extras is almost infinite, of course, but these are some that we have chosen for inclusion on our VW Camper. In some cases, such as the spare wheel carrier, for instance, some versions may not need them because the spare wheel may be carried somewhere else, such as beneath the vehicle. However, the choice is wide, the choice is yours and here's how to go about fitting and applying some of them.

SECTION 1. BODY DECALS

Attractive body decals on the side of the van go a long way towards making it look more of a fun vehicle and less of a work horse. Here are the principles to bear in mind when fitting body decals.

FACT FILE: PREPARATION

• Wash the parts of the vehicle to be fitted with the decals with a detergent, such as washing-up liquid, not car cleaner with body wax.
• Thoroughly wipe all of the areas to which the decals will be applied with panel wipe (available from your local vehicle paint factors), or surgical spirit, available from your local pharmacy. For obvious reasons, **don't** use paint thinner!

6-1-1. Each section of the decal is offered up to the vehicle and marked out so that it can be cut in its correct position.

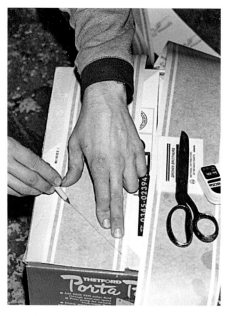

6-1-2. Off the vehicle, the markings are made clear and then cut accurately with scissors.

6-1-3. Use a sponge and water with washing-up liquid in and wet the surface to which the decal is to be applied. Slide the decal onto the surface and use a flat plastic card to squeegee the decal, working from the centre outwards, removing all air bubbles.

Top tips!
• Nothing looks worse than a decal that has been applied at a strange angle!
• You won't be able to get the angle right when you're working close up to the decal.
• Have an assistant look down the length of the decal to make sure that it is parallel to the bodywork and not wavy.
• Stand back and look carefully before moving on to the next stage and check that the decal looks right.

6-1-4. When all the air bubbles have been removed, the backing paper can be peeled off. You'll need to use the wiper to hold the edge being peeled away against the bodywork, as shown here.

6-1-5. You'll also need to press down any lifted-up areas of the decal and carefully ease out any air bubbles that you missed earlier.

Visit Veloce - www.veloce.co.uk

SECTION 2. SWIVELLING PASSENGER SEAT

The following pictures and captions will guide you through the steps involved in this procedure.

6-2-2. Remove the seat as shown in Chapter 5, Section 1. The new swivelling seat base bolts down to the existing seat base runners.

6-2-1. You'll be surprised at how much more versatile the addition of a swivelling passenger seat will make the interior of your Camper. It means that you can have a sociable chat while picnicking, for example, and that someone can easily sit out of the way while their partner prepares food while being on hand to help out when necessary. It makes the seat much easier to use than when you have to squeeze down the central aisle and seems to make the interior of the camper that much bigger. Seat bases are available from Leisuredrive to fit standard VW T3 and T4 seats and from JustKampers for JustKampers' own non-standard seats.

6-2-3. You need to drill three holes in the runners on each side - two at the front and one at the back.

6-2-4. These threaded plates go beneath the front two holes.

6-2-5. The new swivel base is screwed to the threaded plates using special countersunk-head screws provided with the kit.

6-2-6. The seat runners on the swivel base - replicas of the original seat runners - are shown here being lubricated with Wurth's non-staining HSW 100 spray lubricant.

6-2-7. It's easier to refit the seat now because you can swivel the base to one side while sliding the seat into position. When the seat is turned to its straight-ahead position, the swivelling mechanism locks securely. To swivel the seat, you lift a lever beneath the front of the seat and turn - simple as that!

6-3-1. This Apache drive-away awning gave us lots of room on this enjoyable holiday in France. It meant that when we were away, the awning kept our place on the Camping and Caravanning Club site. It gave us room to leave things that would otherwise have had to be carried in the camper when we were out for the day, and it made it so much easier to carry out chores, such as preparing meals or simply getting changed without knocking our elbows on the fixtures and fittings.

SECTION 3. DRIVE-AWAY AWNING

Lots of people use their VW campers for holidays without the addition of an awning but, for a prolonged stay, we've found that the use of our Apache drive-away awning makes a huge difference.

6-3-2. Before setting out to use the awning for the first time, be sure to erect it in the garden at home. It's not difficult, but it is tricky the first time you do it. Once the awning frame was erected in the garden, Shan and I wrapped tape around each joint and put matching letters on them so that it would be far easier to put the thing up on site - and so it proved!

6-3-3. The upper part of the frame is assembled. The legs for the lower part are held to their upper brethren with springs so that they can't come fully apart. The lower part of the legs are folded inwards. This enables you to unroll the canvas in position over the top of the frame.

6-3-4. When this stage is complete, the awning looks like an awning for pixies. Everything is fitted and properly aligned while it's easy to reach at waist or chest height.

6-3-5. You now go round the awning one corner at a time, raising the awning and slotting the lower part of each leg in position.

6-3-6 Apache fits rubber straps all the way around the base of the awning, and these are used for hooking onto the tent pegs which are hammered into the soil.

Top Tip!
• If you buy a tent peg hammer with a hook on the end of it, such as this one from Towsure, you can use it for pulling out tight tent pegs - otherwise tough on the fingers!

6-3-7. There are also four guy ropes, one at each corner of the awning, which need to be fixed to angled tent pegs in the ground. These keep the awning stable and secure in high winds.

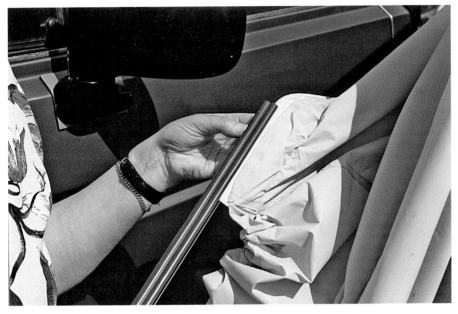

6-3-8. The attachment method that Apache uses for fixing the awning to the motor caravan is an interesting one. The flap which makes the connection between awning and motor caravan has a raised seam on it. Lengths of plastic, like a figure-of-eight but with both sides open, are pushed over the raised seam on the awning flap. Replacements - and different awning attachment systems - are available from JustKampers.

6-3-9. The other ends of the plastic strips are clipped to the drip rail on the side of the camper.

6-3-10. The ends of the flaps are held down with tent pegs adjacent to the corners of the camper.

6-3-11. Inside the awning, you'll need some sort of ground sheet. This is a 'breathable' ground sheet which we purchased from Towsure and is the type specified by some campsites because it causes less damage to the grass.

6-3-12. Colourful curtains come with the Apache awning, and are easily clipped into place. We tend to leave them attached to the awning to make the business of raising and lowering so much quicker.

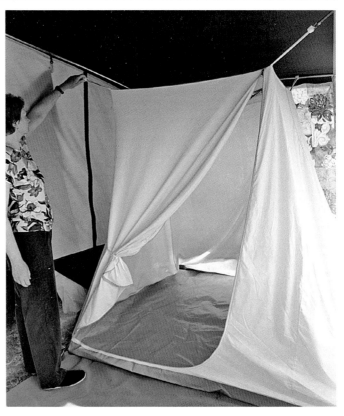

6-3-13. These inner tents are available with the Apache awning and give extra accommodation, should you need it, or a suitably private spot for the chemical toilet.

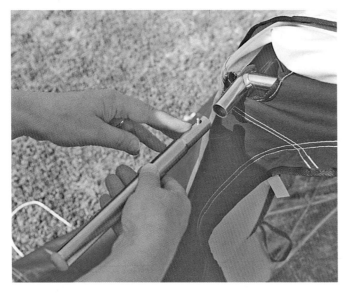

6-3-14. When it's time to take the awning down, note that the poles are held together with these spring-loaded buttons. You have to press them in before the male end of the pole can be removed from the female socket.

6-3-15. It may be tricky to get the Camper back into exactly the right location for connecting the awning flaps. I found an easy way of doing it was to use a piece of white cord held to the ground with a pair of tent pegs. When you drive up, look out of the driver's window, line up the camper with the length of cord and stop at the end tent peg. It's easier than trying to line it up with the awning.

6-3-16. With the camper driven away, the Apache awning can be left closed up with a zipped front door just like any other awning. There's also a separate entrance at the rear for when the camper is connected.

SECTION 4. SILVER SCREEN WINDOW INSULATION

If you've ever been unfortunate enough to have to spend a night in a car, you'll know how cold it gets! One of the main reasons is because of the heat loss through the glass. Since double-glazing is not an option on a vehicle's windscreen, you have to look for another way of keeping the heat in, and the ideal way is to use what have now become generically known as Silver Screens. These are the real McCoy!

6-4-1. The screen for the rear glass hooks over the top of the tailgate and is held at the bottom with straps which pass around the inside of the door.

6-4-2. You shut the tailgate, adjust the Silver Screen, fold the wiper arm back to its normal position and there you are.

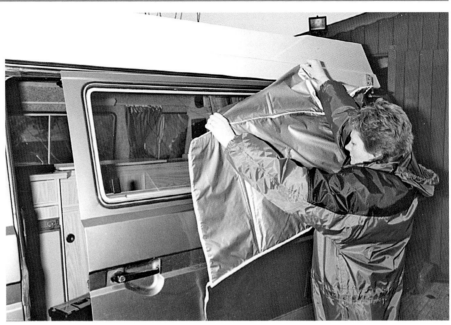

6-4-3. The sliding side door is similarly treated. With the sliding door open, the Silver Screen hooks over the rear of the door ...

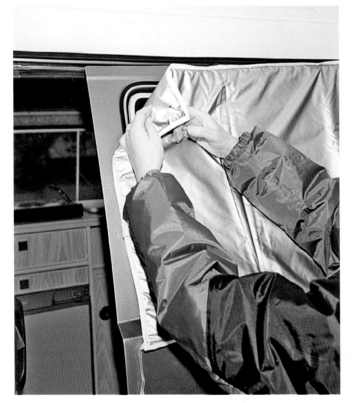

6-4-4. ... and then over the front, and is again tied in place with straps which pass inside the door.

6-4-5. For window glasses that have no visible means of support for the Silver Screens, the screens are fitted with suction pads which adhere to the glass.

6-4-6. The front doors and windscreen - undoubtedly the largest areas of heat loss - are cleverly treated in one go. The screen hooks over the open side door which can then be closed.

6-4-7. With the wipers folded open, the screen is wrapped around the front of the windscreen.

6-4-8. It's then introduced to the other side door which is first opened and then the screen is hooked in place once again. Taking care to spread the tension around the vehicle, this door can also be closed.

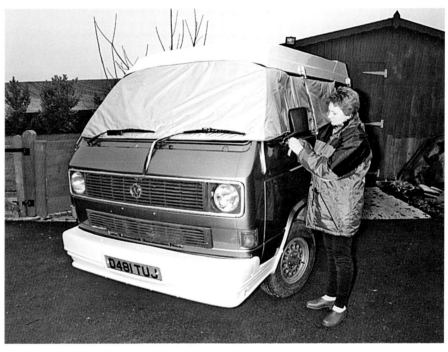

6-4-9. Ties are provided to hold the screen to the wiper arms and the door mirrors. There's now nothing to stop you from opening and closing any of the doors should you need to, and the difference in temperature inside the camper at the time of year these photographs were taken has to be experienced to be believed! An added benefit is that far less condensation will form on the inside of the windows.

SECTION 5. SOLAR PANEL

If your camper is used regularly, the leisure battery will be charged by the vehicle's alternator and it will also be kept charged when you're plugged into the mains on site via the Zig unit described earlier in this manual. However, if you use a site without mains electricity, or if your camper is parked up for long periods of time, you can keep the leisure battery topped up by using a solar panel on the roof. This Exide panel is no longer available in the UK at the time of writing because, for reasons best known to itself, Exide has withdrawn from the leisure side of the market which it only recently entered. Still, other makes are available - see advertisements in the caravan and motor caravan magazines.

6-5-2. This 15 watt panel will be too much for the battery if it's left permanently connected. In fact, it will rapidly destroy it. For that reason, you need a battery controller which will only allow charge to reach the battery when it needs it and cut it off when the battery is fully charged. The right sort of controller will also control the output from the battery and prevent the battery from being fully drained.

6-5-1. There's an ideal spot on the top of the Leisuredrive elevating roof for siting the solar panel, provided you don't want to carry luggage up there - which we don't. The panel simply screws down to the timber-reinforced section of the roof but you have to be sure to seal each of the mounting holes, and the hole through which the cable needs to pass, with suitable silicone sealant.

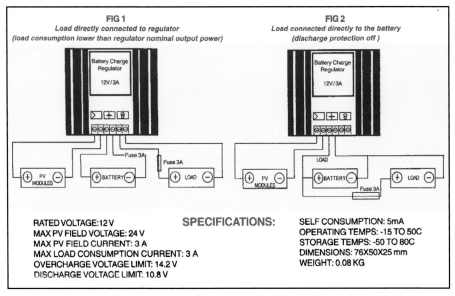

FIG 1
Load directly connected to regulator
(load consumption lower than regulator nominal output power)

FIG 2
Load connected directly to the battery
(discharge protection off)

SPECIFICATIONS:

RATED VOLTAGE: 12 V
MAX PV FIELD VOLTAGE: 24 V
MAX PV FIELD CURRENT: 3 A
MAX LOAD CONSUMPTION CURRENT: 3 A
OVERCHARGE VOLTAGE LIMIT: 14.2 V
DISCHARGE VOLTAGE LIMIT: 10.8 V

SELF CONSUMPTION: 5mA
OPERATING TEMPS: -15 TO 50C
STORAGE TEMPS: -50 TO 80C
DIMENSIONS: 76X50X25 mm
WEIGHT: 0.08 KG

6-5-3. These are typical connections for using the charge controller. As with other electrical components, you will need to have a qualified electrician make these connections for you.

SECTION 6. SPARE WHEEL CARRIER

The following pictures and captions will guide you through the steps involved in this procedure.

6-6-1. Where a spare wheel is normally carried inside the vehicle, a spare wheel carrier can make a huge amount of difference to the space you have available. Alternatively, if a spare wheel is carried beneath the vehicle and you have it converted to run on LPG, or you have underfloor tanks where the spare wheel would normally go, this type of spare wheel carrier, supplied by Leisuredrive, gives you further options.

6-6-2. The first job is to assemble the individual components in the kit using the parts list supplied.

6-6-3. Leisuredrive's Barry starts by establishing the correct location for the spare wheel carrier brackets, with reference to the dimensions shown in the instructions. The positioning is absolutely critical.

6-6-4. Both hinge brackets take an awful lot of strain so plates with captive nuts are supplied and these have to be located inside the rear pillars. It's an extremely tight fit to get your arm inside the pillar to hold the plates in place, even after removing the air intake ducting which passes through this part of the pillar. Still, there's nothing else for it.

6-6-5. Barry carefully drills pilot holes and then clearance holes for the bolts used for fitting the hinge to the pillar.

Top tip!
• When drilling, Barry uses a block of wood with a clearance (i.e. larger) hole drilled down the middle of it as a stop to prevent the drill from damaging the far side of the bodywork as it breaks through the hole in the pillar.

6-6-6. Bare metal is primed and painted to stop it from rusting.

6-6-7. At this stage, the hinge is temporarily held in place and the bolts just pushed through the holes to make sure that they locate properly. The positions of the holes that have to be drilled through the insides of the pillar are now marked and pilot holes drilled. Note the wooden block, pre-drilled with a clearance hole, used as a stop to prevent the drill from damaging the outer body panel.

6-6-8. A suitable silicone sealant is applied to the hinge bracket ...

6-6-9. ... which can then be bolted in place.

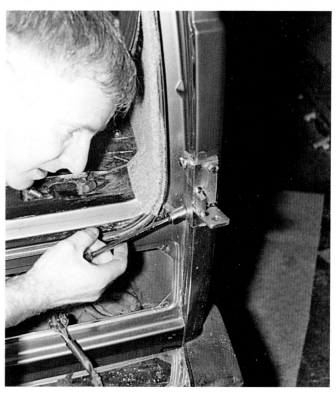

6-6-10. The same procedure is followed for the lower hinge bracket although access for the nut plate is far easier because all you have to do is remove the rear light unit.

6-6-11. Barry and Roy fit the frame to the hinge mechanism and then mark out the exact location for the catch which fits on the rear door.

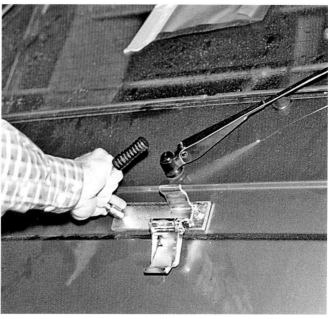

6-6-12. The catch also takes quite a lot of stress and is bolted through the door, after taking off the interior trim, using the nut plate provided.

6-6-13. The frame itself is adjustable after slackening these locknuts and bolts.

6-6-14. Start off by adjusting it a touch high ...

6-6-15. ... so that when the spare wheel is fitted, the frame slots accurately into the catch on the rear door. If the weight of the spare wheel moves the frame by more or less than you predicted, simply slacken the adjuster bolts and adjust the position once again.

SECTION 7. TOW BRACKET

One of the first jobs we carried out was to fit a Brink tow bracket to the rear of the Transporter.

6-7-1. When we go away, this small Towsure Caddy trailer with a hinged rigid roof is perfect for loading in the awning and for bringing back the wine!

6-7-2. We were very impressed by the quality and comprehensiveness of the Brink tow bracket and the Ryder International electrical kit. While we were doing the job, we wired in a supplementary caravan socket just in case we ever wanted to pull a caravan. This enables a leisure battery on a caravan to be charged as you drive along. Obviously, it makes the job a lot more complex than connecting in a tow bracket and wiring assembly for towing a simple trailer because then all you need to do is tap into the lighting circuits.

6-7-3. You remove the rear bumper and also the bumper mounting brackets from the chassis.

6-7-4. The tow bracket, which includes mountings for the bumper, fits in place of the original mounting bracket. This is then bolted to the chassis.

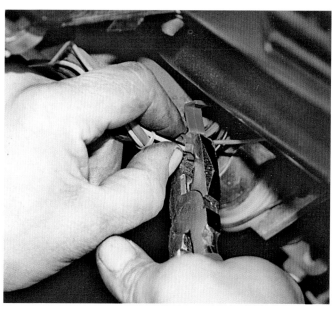

6-7-5. Because caravan wiring was being installed, some of the wiring had to be connected to the loom beneath the steering column. In this location it's okay to use Scotchlok connectors because they're not exposed to damp. At the rear of the vehicle, where connections may be exposed to damp, you are strongly advised to use soldered or crimped bullet or spade connectors.

6-7-6. The Ryder wiring kit includes a relay to prevent current being provided to a caravan battery when the engine isn't running - essential if you don't want to drain your tow vehicle's main battery.

6-7-7. Later on, the Brink tow bracket was modified to take a height-adjustable Land Rover-type tow bracket, this one from Witter. (This isn't needed on non-Syncro Transporters with their standard ride height.) You need to be an accomplished welder to carry out this sort of work safely because the strength of a tow bracket is all-important, and this was a process of combining the Volkswagen bracket with a Land Rover rear end.

6-7-8. Because the bottom of the replacement bracket came much lower than the original bracket, a pair of strong locating straps were made up and connected to the underside of the vehicle.

6-7-9. This one-off tow bracket fouled the bumper which had to be modified as shown here. The bottom of the bumper must be cut away to clear the bracket.

6-7-10. The cut edges of the bumper were painted with zinc primer and then silver gloss to prevent any corrosion from taking a hold.

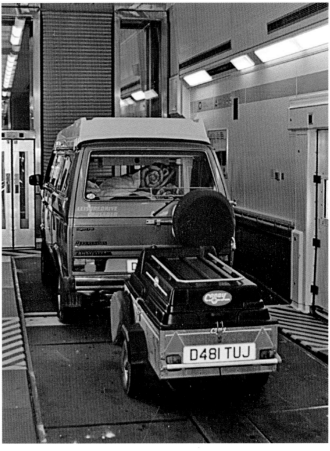

6-7-11. When the Caddy trailer isn't connected for a trip through Eurotunnel, it's used for taking rubbish down to the tip rather than risk damaging the inside of our lovely camper!

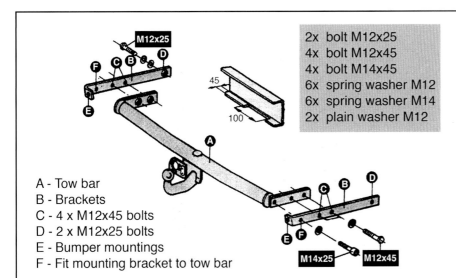

2x bolt M12x25
4x bolt M12x45
4x bolt M14x45
6x spring washer M12
6x spring washer M14
2x plain washer M12

6-7-12. This is the layout of the components supplied for the Brink towbracket for the T3.

A - Tow bar
B - Brackets
C - 4 x M12x45 bolts
D - 2 x M12x25 bolts
E - Bumper mountings
F - Fit mounting bracket to tow bar

SECTION 8. FITTING A FRONT SPOILER

T4 owners can stop reading here because, unless they're going for cosmetic looks, an auxiliary front spoiler won't be necessary. T3 owners may find that their vehicle is not as stable at high speed on the motorway as they would wish, especially with a high-top roof. Leisuredrive can make this fibreglass spoiler to order in its fibreglass workshop and I can tell you that it makes a real difference to the stability of the vehicle at motorway speeds.

6-8-1. The strongly-built front spoiler comes out of the mould in the Leisuredrive factory.

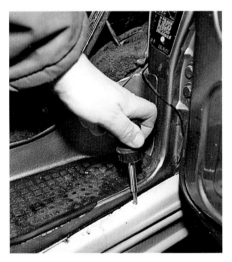

6-8-2. The spoiler fits over the existing bumper and you need to drill your own holes in both spoiler and bumper for locating the two together. I used screw caps, available from the local DIY store, rather than leaving screwheads visible.

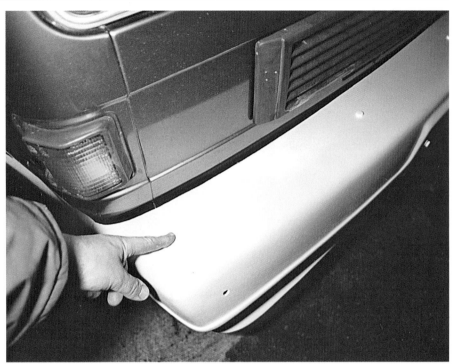

6-8-3. You always have to do a little trimming on fibreglass spoilers of this sort, although not a great deal was needed in this case. The spoiler fits at the bottom of the doorstep and the front of the wheelarch where it is once again screwed into place. I used stainless steel screws to prevent any risk of corrosion.

6-8-4. One of the down-sides of a spoiler is that it is prone to being broken if it catches on a kerb. I made up a reinforcer to help prevent this from happening. Straps fit to the front undertray retaining bolts and a piece of channel was carefully bent (across my knee), to follow the exact shape of the spoiler.

6-8-5. Once bolted in place, you can see the extra strength imparted by my simple modification.

6-8-6. Later on, the spoiler was painted but it already gives an attractive appearance to the front of the camper as well as having true practical value.

SECTION 9. FITTING POWER STEERING TO A T3 TRANSPORTER

Most T3s, especially in Europe, come without power steering and that can make them hard work. Converting them to power steering is not a job for the faint hearted, and it's a relatively expensive modification to carry out, too. There are one or two cost-saving steps you can take and they are discussed here.

SAFETY FIRST!
• Note that the vehicle must always be supported both by a trolley jack and by axle stands.
• You must never go beneath a vehicle supported only by a jack.

6-9-1. On the T3, the steering column goes forwards to an angle drive box and then a supplementary column goes back to the steering rack. The first job is to remove this steering shaft from the vehicle. It's made all the more difficult on this one by the fitting of an LPG gas tank.

6-9-2. This is the manual steering rack which has been unbolted from the vehicle. There are four mounting bolt holes, two of which are shown here (arrowed). You can also see the shock-absorbent rag joint which is taken off the spline on the steering column, and which has to be replaced with the power steering system's universal joint at the rack end only. It's best to buy a new one of these because they do tend to wear.

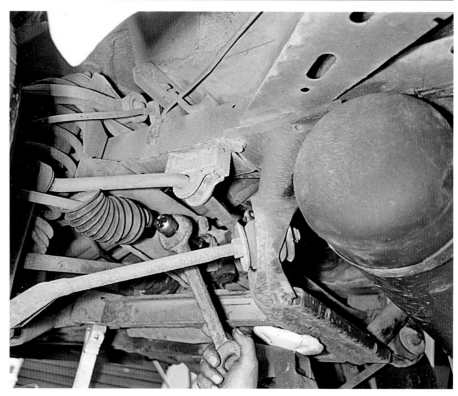

6-9-3. Taking a step back now, this is the connection between the end of the steering rack and the steering arm which goes to the hub on the vehicle. The steering arms are reused with the new rack so you can unscrew one from the other from underneath the vehicle.

6-9-4. A new steering rack from Volkswagen would cost you an arm and several legs. An alternative is to buy one from ZF, the manufacturer of the steering racks. This is what I did and it saved an awful lot of money as well as providing me with some excellent service. ZF in the UK was able to advise on precisely which rack I would need. The rack was fitted with new mounting bushes, seals, gaiters and pipe mounting adaptors.

6-9-5. After removing the blanking plugs, the pipe mounting bushes were wrapped around with PTFF tape - always use in the opposite direction to that which you screw the thread in - to make sure that the thread will seal under pressure.

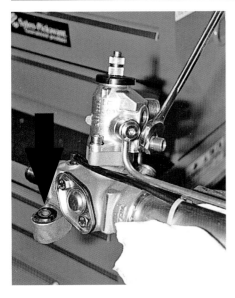

6-9-6. The new fittings were screwed into the new rack. As you can see, the rack mounting bushes (arrowed) have already been fitted. Use lubricant, such as washing-up liquid, to help push them in.

6-9-7. The new rack is fitted to the underside of the vehicle using the original nuts, washers and bolts.

6-9-8. The new universal joint is fitted to the spline on the power steering rack and also on the shaft that goes forward to connect to the steering column.

6-9-9. You also have to fit a new shaft - the one from the old system won't do - and a new rag joint being pointed out here.

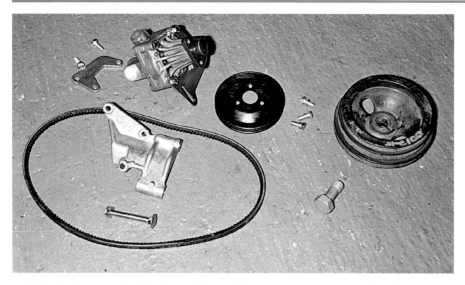

6-9-10. Here's a range of parts that you will also need in order to carry out the conversion. All except one were purchased from Volkswagen and we'll come to that in a moment. The parts, reading in a clockwise direction from the top left-hand corner, are:
1. Pump mounting bracket and bolts. 2. Power steering pump. 3. Pump pulley and mounting bolts.
4. Crankshaft pulley. 5. Crankshaft pulley bolt (you'll also need a new seal to go on the back of the crankshaft pulley). 6. Drive belt. 7. Large pump mounting bracket and swivel bolt.
All of the parts were available at the time of writing, at quite a reasonable price from a Volkswagen dealer, except for the crankshaft pulley, which was astoundingly expensive! As you can see, this pulley is not a new one. I found a Volkswagen Transporter breaker in California by searching on the internet, telephoned him (much to his surprise), and had it mailed to me, all for about $50.00. The wonders of the internet! I'm sure that other components, such as pulleys and brackets, would also have been available in the same way, but as they were reasonably priced, I purchased new. The pump itself was, in comparison with the other parts, surprisingly inexpensive, and this is probably because it is a common part used on other Volkswagen vehicles.

6-9-11. To fit the new pump, you have to remove the alternator.

6-9-12. The pump mounting bracket is bolted to existing threaded holes on the engine.

6-9-13. The bracket and pulley are fitted to the new pump.

6-9-14. In our case, the oil seal ring had to be removed from the back of the now redundant crank pulley ...

6-9-15. ... and pressed into place on the 'new' Californian pulley.

6-9-16. You need to fit a new bolt (from VW) when mounting the wider pulley in place because of the extra length of bolt needed. Don't be tempted to use the old bolt because it won't be sufficiently secure.

6-9-17. There's only just room to manoeuvre the new pulley onto the crank nose between the engine and the bodywork.

6-9-18. Lock the engine, using a locking pin, to prevent it from turning.

6-9-19. The pulley can now be bolted to the crank using a large spanner. Ideally, you would use a torque wrench but, in our case, there wasn't enough room to fit one in. We just made sure it was bl***y tight!

6-9-20. The pump and belt can now be fitted and the belt tensioned as described in the manual. If you are mystified by some of the other pipework in the engine bay, it's because it's part of the LPG gas system which, incidentally, suits this engine wonderfully well.

6-9-21. I went to a Volkswagen breaker and found a suitable Passat power steering pump reservoir for the engine bay.

6-9-22. The power steering pipework - and we'll deal with that in a moment - has to be bolted to the rack ...

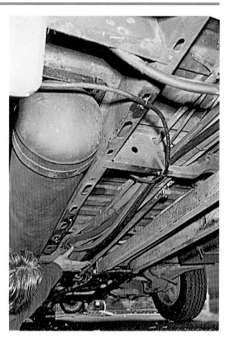

6-9-23. ... and the pipework passed down the length of the vehicle.

Important note: The correct Volkswagen pipework is, once again, horrendously expensive, and it wouldn't have been practicable to have had it shipped from 6000 miles away. I had new pipes made up at my local agricultural engineers, using high pressure hydraulic pipework capable of carrying loads far greater than those required by the power steering system. These flexible hoses have the added advantage that they were more easily routed underneath the vehicle, but they did have to be carefully tied into place because of their lack of rigidity.

6-9-24. At the front of the vehicle, the new hoses were bolted to the pump and, later, to the power steering reservoir as required.

6-9-25. The correct power steering fluid is Borg-Warner ATF (automatic transmission fluid).

SECTION 10. FITTING A SCORPION ALARM
The following pictures and captions will guide you through the steps involved in this procedure.

6-10-2. David is working underneath the front end of the vehicle with the undertray removed. This vehicle has been converted to run on LPG, so the large canister you can see - not normally fitted to Transporters, of course - is the gas tank. David has decided to fit the siren into this well protected area and is drilling through the floor so that he can lead cables directly into the dash.

6-10-1. We fitted a Scorpion 1014T2 unit to our project Camper. Scorpion's David Seale recommended this particular unit because it is one of the most effective Category One alarms around. All of the electronics are combined in the siren and immobiliser units, making for compact installation and less for the potential thief to get hold of. Category One systems have the highest insurance rating in the UK and incorporate both an immobiliser and a siren alarm, whereas Category Two systems comprise just an immobiliser. Both are passively armed - which means that the unit turns itself on automatically when you leave the vehicle.

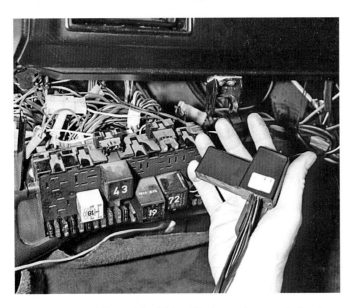

6-10-3. The immobiliser unit itself is best fitted somewhere near the fuse box and, of course, there's plenty of room at the front end of the Transporter.

6-10-4. Fitting the wiring would be a nightmare to the non-expert - there is just so much of it! - but David neatly spliced the Scorpion alarm's loom into the vehicle's wiring loom.

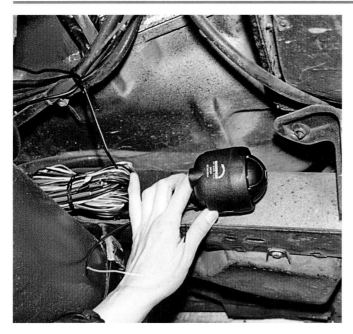

6-10-5. With the immobiliser in place, David found a dry, well protected area - well away from the obvious places for a thief to look - for the battery backed-up siren unit. Again, you can see a dauntingly large amount of wiring which has to be connected. In order for an alarm to receive acceptance by an insurance company, it has to be installed by an approved fitter, so this part of the work is hardly a DIY job.

6-10-6. All of the doors are protected by wiring connected into the courtesy light switches. On models without courtesy light switches, it's necessary to fit contact switches of an appropriate type.

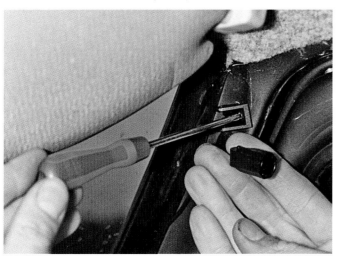

6-10-7. David also fitted movement sensors to the tops of the windscreen pillars. Unlike with some systems, these sensors are mounted on neat brackets which are screwed to the pillars so that they are held securely in place. The downside of this set-up is that the movement sensors would be concealed if you were to close the curtains and leave the vehicle. On the other hand, if you wanted to alarm the system while you were sleeping in the vehicle, you could do so while disarming the internal sensors, using a secondary button on the remote control key fob. In this instance, it wouldn't matter whether the sensors were covered up by the curtains or not, obviously!

6-10-8. David had to find somewhere prominent on the dash to fit the warning light. Adjacent to the warning light, David also fitted the optional extra, touch-key socket.

6-10-9. If you should accidentally lose or damage your remote control or the batteries fail while you are away from the vehicle, the touch-key socket will be a godsend! The beauty of this system is that without the remote control, you can still get into the vehicle and disarm it. It is not possible for a thief to short-out the touch-key socket because of the random re-coding which the socket shares with the remote control.

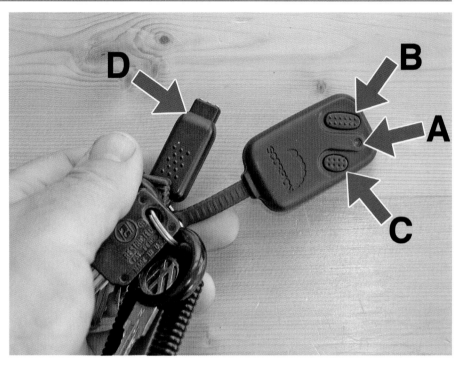

6-10-10. The Scorpion remote pad has two buttons and an LED light (A). One button (B) disarms the alarm, while the other (C) is used as a 'panic' button - in other words, when you press it within the vicinity of the vehicle, the alarm goes off in the hope that you will frighten off any would-be attacker - and the panic button is also used as a supplementary button for disarming the internal sensors, should you wish to do so. The smaller of the items on this keyring (D) is the touch-key shown in the earlier shot.

SECTION 11. LOCKING WHEEL NUTS

If you have fitted good-looking alloy wheels to your pride and joy, you will want to protect them as best you can.

6-11-1. You may also want to replace tired-looking Volkswagen wheel nuts. Be sure that the ones you buy for replacement have exactly the same angle of taper, and that the thread length inside the nut is the same as that on the original.

6-10-11. The Scorpion stickers placed on the side windows combine with the warning light on the dash to let the thief know that a top-brand alarm system is fitted and armed so, if he really wants to steal a vehicle, he should go somewhere else!

6-11-2. We found that Paddy Hopkirk in the UK supplies McGard wheel locks. They come in a handy re-usable package for storing the key tool and spare wheel nuts.

6-11-3. It's important that alloy wheels - in fact all wheels - are tightened with a torque wrench and that the tension is checked regularly. You should never use an air wrench on plated nuts, in fact, they're a bad idea anyway because you can't judge the torque correctly. It's worth remembering that over-tightened nuts can be at least as dangerous as under-tightened ones and it is, therefore, essential to tighten the wheel nuts to the figures shown in your vehicle handbook.

SECTION 12. T3 NUDGE BAR

There's a lot of controversy over the use of nudge bars - sometimes known as bull bars - because of their potential for causing injury to pedestrians in an accident. On balance, I feel that they're a good idea on the T3 Transporter because of the fact that there's no engine there, and the driver and passenger are 'close to the accident' and need all the protection they can get. I don't think there's any justification for fitting them to T4 models, however.

6-12-1. In our case, a spoiler was fitted and it was necessary to cut a slot in the spoiler in order to fit the nudge bar.

6-12-2. The nudge bar bolts to the front chassis and needs to be held in position while it is fitted. An engine crane was found to be useful to carry the weight of the nudge bar.

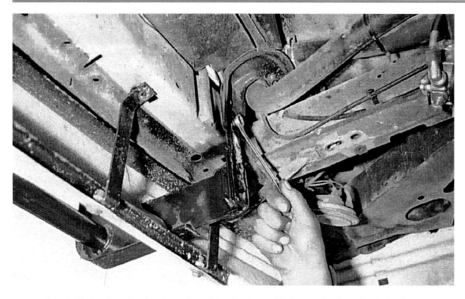

6-12-3. Bolting it to the chassis at the points already provided proved to be a simple business.

SECTION 13. MAINS TESTER

The Zig unit fitted to our caravan has a double-pole switch so, in theory, it shouldn't matter which way round the positive and negative terminals on the mains are connected. On the Continent, two-pin plugs and sockets often have no means of ensuring that they are connected the correct way round and this is because Continental caravans tend to have double-pole circuitry fitted as standard. However, to be on the safe side, it's far better if you ensure that the mains coming into your camper is connected up correctly: positive-to-positive and negative-to-negative.

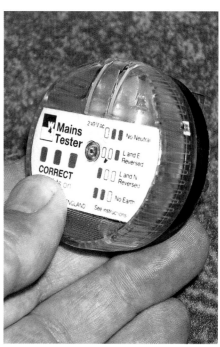

6-13-1. To check the mains, you will need a mains tester, such as the unit shown here. You will also be able to buy a short length of cable with a switched-over plug and socket to reverse the polarity for those sites where the connections are the 'wrong' way round. The result of having an unprotected positive-to-negative supply could easily prove fatal.

6-12-4. It was necessary to remove the grille and to drill the grille surround in order to fix the steadying plates at this position. These screws tend to come undone so it's a good idea to use lockwashers under their heads.

SECTION 14. CARBON MONOXIDE ALARM

A smoke alarm is a useful thing to have, but a carbon monoxide (or CO) alarm has probably got even more practical benefit. Best of all, fit both!

6-14-1. A CO alarm will tell you if the level of carbon monoxide in the enclosed space that makes up your Camper is becoming too high - something that can happen if combustion gases from any of the appliances are exhausted into the interior of the Camper rather than outside as a result of damage or blockages of which you may be unaware. There's no special installation required for a carbon monoxide alarm, you just have to be sure that the alarm is not situated in place where air won't circulate, and that, conversely, it's not situated where there is lots of fresh-air ventilation which could distort its true reading.

SECTION 15. PORTABLE TOILET

The Thetford Porta Potti, with its flush-water tank mounted above the waste tank, is perfect for VW Camper-sized motor caravans.

Important note: If water is left in the flushing tank, it could freeze in the winter and ruin the Porta Potti. Be sure to drain the flushing tank if there is any risk of it freezing in the winter months.

6-15-2. To empty a Porta Potti, you slide the latch to one side while simultaneously removing the water tank from the waste tank. Note that when the flush water tank is removed from the waste tank, the valve handle locks.

6-15-1. The ideal place for locating the Thetford Porta Potti is in this cupboard built in to part of the bed box. Leisuredrive makes the cupboard so that the Porta Potti is a snug fit and can't bang around in there as the vehicle is cornering.
As an alternative, Leisuredrive can fit a small cupboard just inside the sliding door, behind the passenger seat. This provides a small seat on the lid when it's closed and access to the Porta Potti when the lid is open. It prevents you from having a swivelling passenger seat, of course.

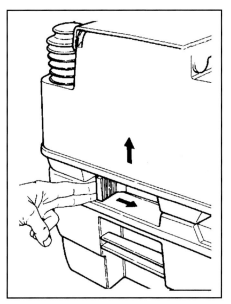

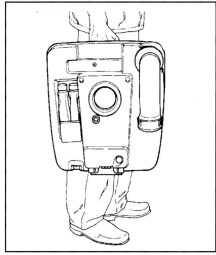

6-15-3. The waste tank can be carried to the disposal point using the integral carrying handle.

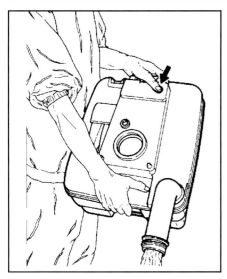

6-15-4. Place the waste tank on end with the carrying handle uppermost and swivel the pour-out spout so that it is facing upwards. Remove the cap and, as you pour the waste away, depress the vent plunger (arrowed). This allows the waste to come out in a steady stream instead of 'glugging' and splashing over you.

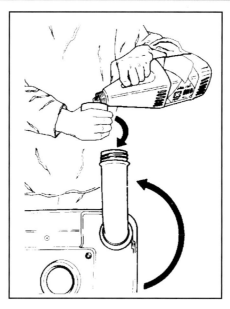

6-15-5. Pour approximately two litres of water into the waste holding tank and add an appropriate amount of toilet fluid. On some models, the cap doubles as a measuring cup; on others, use the measures shown on the bottle of fluid.

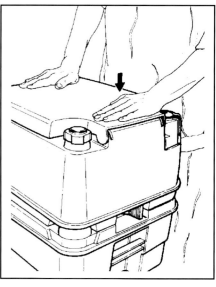

6-15-6. With the cap back on the pour-out spout and the spout twisted back into position, place the waste tank on its base. The water tank can now be placed squarely on top of the waste tank and pushed down until the latching system locks the two tanks together.

SAFETY FIRST!

• Keep all toilet chemicals out of the reach of small children. It's advisable to wear protective gloves when using the fluid and if any comes into contact with your eyes, wash them immediately with cold water and seek medical advice.

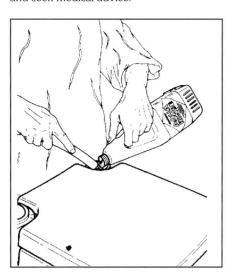

6-15-7. Remove the cap of the flush-water tank and fill the tank with clean water. Add the appropriate amount of toilet rinse and replace the cap.

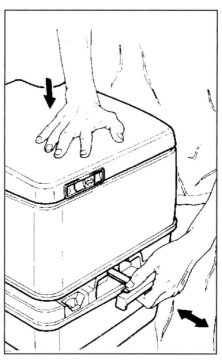

6-15-8. In order to prevent any pressure build-up, hold the lid closed and open and close the waste tank valve blade once.

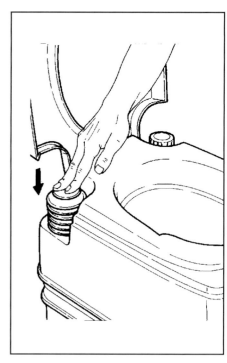

6-15-9. Before using the toilet, press the pump (or the pump button on electric models), so that there is a little flushing water in the bowl.

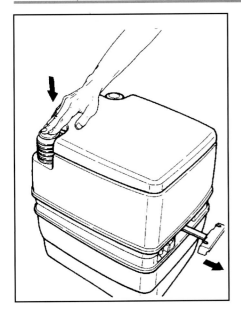

6-15-10. After using the toilet, open the valve blade by pulling out the valve handle. Now flush the toilet by pressing the pump or the pump button (three to four short, sharp flushes are recommended with electric models), then close the valve.

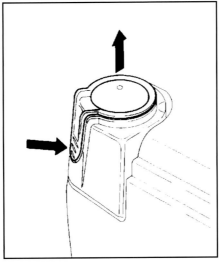

6-15-11. On electric models, alkaline batteries are usually good for 500 to 600 flushes. When there is not enough power to pump through enough water to cover the toilet bowl completely, the batteries should be replaced. Depress the latch of the battery housing and pull the housing upwards and out of the pump.

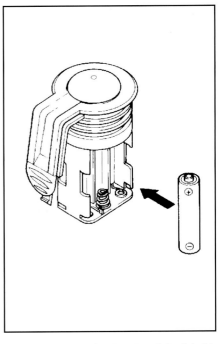

6-15-12. The battery housing takes six Penlight/AA 1.4/1.5 alkaline batteries, as shown.

Chapter 7
Specialists, tools & equipment

This chapter shows much of the equipment and many of the tools to be used when carrying out the work described in this manual. It also lists the specialists whose services we have used, and others I can recommend. The list does not attempt to be exhaustive; it's a list of people and equipment I have used, know about and have found useful. At the same time, none of this is advertising on the part of the companies featured here. I hope you find the information helpful.

Apache, C.G.I. Camping, PO Box 373, Newcastle, Staffs, ST5 3TD
Tel: 01782 713 099
www.apachetents.com

Autopaint International, Autopaint House, Marl Road, Knowsley Industrial Park, Knowsley, Merseyside, L33 7UM
Tel: 0151 549 1409
www.autopaint.co.uk

7-1. The French know a thing or two about tents, and a drive-away Apache awning is the perfect way of giving you extra room to stretch those arms and legs. It also allows you to reserve your pitch when you drive away and gives you somewhere to leave your stuff when you're not on site.

7-2. Most paint manufacturers won't supply to 'the public' but Autopaint will. Our Camper has been finished using these materials.

7-3. If you need a specific shade to be matched, it can be mixed for you at one of Autopaint's local centres.

Autopaint supplies a full range of cellulose paint (which it is possible to use at home, with appropriate safety equipment and precautions), and 2-pack paint, which is strictly for professional paint shops only, plus all ancillaries.

Brink UK Ltd, Unit 7, Centrovell Industrial Estate, Caldwell Road, Nuneaton, Warks, CV11 4NG
Tel: 01203 352 353
www.brink-towbars.co.uk

7-4. It's not easy to buy a purpose-made towbar for a T3 Transporter but Brink manufactures a very good quality one. Unfortunately, the towball height is somewhat too high when fitted to a Syncro.

Burco Dean Appliances Ltd, Rose Grove, Burnley, Lancs, BB12 6AL
Tel: 01282 427 241
www.burcodean.com

7-5. The Malaga and Malaga E water heater range is among the classics of the caravan and motor caravan world. It's really great to be able to have hot water on tap even in a camper of this size.

7-6. Transporters have plenty of room underneath them for fitting water storage tanks. CAK Tanks manufactures tanks in every shape and size as well as retailing just about the complete range of motor caravan accessories.

CAK Tanks Ltd, 10 Princes Drive, Kenilworth, Warks, CV8 2FD
Tel: 01926 854 271

Clarke International Ltd, Hemnall Street, Epping, Essex, CM16 4LG

7-7. For cutting out side-windows and for cutting timber panels, you'll need a jigsaw. It's one of the tools that you really can't do without. This is the CJS2 model with the more powerful 420 watt motor.

Tel: 01992 565 300
www.clarkeinternational.com

Clarke's range of power tools is probably second-to-none in the UK. There are branches of Machine Mart all around the UK from which all Clarke tools can be purchased. We use Clarke tools extensively in our workshop and here is a small selection of those used in this manual.

7-8. The CAT26B air-powered saw is lightning fast but might be too fierce in inexperienced hands. The CAT63 'air nibbler' would be a better bet for those who have an air compressor.

7-9. Another must-have tool, if you're carrying out any bodywork repairs, will be a 4½in angle grinder. You can then handle all those grinding jobs, such as cleaning up welds or other rough areas of metal, but it can also be used with cutting or sanding discs. This one is fitted with a powerful wire brush.

7-10. Compressors are used for a whole range of jobs, as well as powering air tools. You can do your own paint spraying, blow up tyres, inject rustproofing fluids (the correct way!) and blow dust out of cavities (always wear goggles) - the list is endless, if you're serious about vehicle DIY. There is a huge range of Clarke models - best to go and take a look at them to find out which one best suits your needs. And remember, apart from the obvious considerations of cost and space, you can never have too large a compressor because you can't have too much compressed air; only too little!

7-11. If you buy one of these then, like me, you'll justify buying it for the Camper but with a view to using it all round the paths and garden. (Or vice versa, depending on where your priorities lie!) The Jet 5000 Power Washer can be used for cleaning the van's underside, the interior before conversion and the exterior afterwards, though you have to take care not to pull too hard on the hose or it will topple over.

7-12. You'll need a range of workshop tools, from spanners to hammers; hacksaws to vice-jaws. Most of us have collected 'odd' items together over the years, but you can find the full range on the Machine Mart web site: www.machinemart.co.uk

7-13. If you take your Camper to lots of out-of-the-way places, you'll find a small compressor a boon. This is yours truly 'borrowing' the Clarke Power 700W generator from the Camper to use an electric drill away from an easy source of mains power.

7-16. The Dunlop 'Fill & Go' kit enables you to correct tyre pressures with a seriously effective pump operated from the cigarette lighter, with the reassuring addition of an emergency sealant for use in the case of punctures. Fill & Go enables you to reflate a tyre sufficiently to continue your journey at reduced speed and then, when the tyre is removed from the wheel, it easily washes out, unlike some similar substances which adhere to and ruin the tyre.

Cotswold Motor Spares (4.W.D.) Ltd, 18 Elliott Road, Love Lane Industrial Estate, Cirencester, Glos, GL7 1YS
Tel: 01285 658 015
Supplier of the nudge bar fitted to our project T3 Camper.

Dometic, 99 Oakley Road, Luton, Beds, LU4 9GE
Tel: 01582 494 111
www.dometic.co.uk

Dunlop Tyres Ltd, TyreFort, 88-98 Wingfoot Way, Birmingham, B24 9HY
Tel: 0121 306 6000
www.dunloptyres.co.uk

Holden Vintage & Classic, Linton Trading Estate, Bromyard, Hfds, HR7 4QT
Tel: 01885 488 000
www.holden.co.uk

As the name suggests, Holden sets out primarily to serve the classic car market. But the number of parts, large and small; consumables, materials and accessories, have to be seen to be believed. See its catalogues - expensive but better produced than most magazines - or the web site, to see what I mean.

J & M Designs (Silver Screens), 'Broadgates', Bank Street, Cleckheaton, West Yorkshire, BD19 5EP
Tel: 01274 872 151

7-14. For years Dometic was known as Electrolux and it still produces the famous range of fridges - constantly being revised and improved, of course, - fitted to generations of caravans and campers.

7-15. Dunlop's 'commercial' tyre range includes the ideal tyre for a VW Camper. And you really do need heavy-duty tyres and not ordinary car tyres because of the weights that the tyres have to bear. I found that these tyres have provided an excellent, quiet ride and have worn better than any car tyres I have used - I suppose they're expected to for the commercial market.

7-17. These are the original and arguably the best insulators for keeping the cold out and the warm in.

7-18. JP Exhausts stainless steel systems are the best-quality stainless sytems - both for fit and build quality - that this author has seen. TIP: Use stainless clamps with threadlock to prevent nuts from coming unscrewed.

7-19. JustKampers attends all the VW shows and sells a great range of T3 and T4 spares.

JP Exhausts, Old School House, Brook Street, Macclesfield, Cheshire, SK11 7AW
Tel: 01625 619 916
www.jpexhausts.co.uk

JustKampers, Unit 1, Stapeley Manor, Long Lane, Odiham, Hants, RG29 1JE
Tel: 01256 862 288
www.justkampers.co.uk
JustKampers isn't the only specialist dealing in Transporter - and, unsurprisingly, Camper - parts. But it is by far the biggest and with the widest range of parts you could wish for. You can buy all your servicing and repair requirements as well as a huge range of holiday and leisure equipment requirements from JustKampers. The Katalogue (it would be, wouldn't it!) is a treasure trove, and the web site is well worth adding to your list of 'Favourites'.

Leisuredrive, 10 Corporation Street, Manchester, M4 4DG
Tel: 0161 819 2220
www.leisuredrive.co.uk
Without Leisuredrive, this manual would not exist. The company carried out all of the work shown on these pages and was happy to spend as much time as was needed to make sure that everything was properly photographed. Obviously, the publicity was always going to be desirable, but I can't speak too highly of the professionalism of the guys in the workshop and the helpfulness of everyone at the company. A word of warning. If you visit Leisuredrive's premises in Manchester and look around the surroundings, you won't be impressed! But if you wanted to have an atrium, you'd have to pay for it in the price of the finished product. Leisuredrive's conversions, whether carried out on new vans or used, are solid, honest, hard

wearing and good value. They're not the lightest in weight, not the trendiest decor but, from what I've seen in the weeks I've spent making a pest of myself at the Leisuredrive workshops, the motorcaravan conversions are honest, well built - and you don't half save a lot of dosh!

Morris Lubricants, Castle Foregate, Shrewsbury, Shropshire, SY1 2EL
Tel: 01743 232 200

www.morrislubricants.co.uk

NC Interiors, Tel: 01204 793 335
NC Interiors makes all the trim for Leisuredrive's conversions - and does a smashing job!

Optima Batteries, BYC House, Birdhan, Chichester, West Sussex, PO20 7BB
Tel: 01243 514 214
www.optimabattery.co.uk

7-20. Leisuredrive has been converting motor caravans for many years. The latest designs are still fresh and attractive-looking and Leisuredrive is a widely recognised brand when it comes to insuring or reselling the vehicle.

7-21. My company, Porter Manuals, uses Morris Lubricants in preference to any other. For one thing, Morris is Britain's largest independent manufacturer of lubricants and, for another, it's darned good stuff without being over-expensive.

7-23. For everyday cars, everyday batteries are fine. But campers need batteries that can withstand more punishment. Optima batteries are more expensive than most but are much longer-lasting, better at starting your car and can be recharged in an hour. New battery technology!

Paddy Hopkirk Ltd, Eden Way, Pages Industrial Park, Leighton Buzzard, Bedfordshire, LU7 8TZ
Tel: 01525 850 800

7-22. MacGuard wheel nuts are an essential fitment where expensive wheels and tyres are concerned.

Andy Price, Allan Legge & Sons, Butterley Cottage, Thornbury, Nr. Bromyard, Hfds, HR7 4NG
Tel: 01885 482 302

7-24. Andy sprays all of our vehicles and his work on our Transporter has been up to his usual very high standard.

Propex Marketing Ltd, Unit 5, Second
Avenue Business Park, Millbrook,
Southampton, SO15 0LT
Tel: 01703 528 555
www.propexheatsource.co.uk

7-25. We fitted one of the first of Propex's new blown-air heaters to our camper and it's proved to be extremely useful for winter picnics as well as for camping.

7-26. If you're just popping out for the day and don't want to bother firing up the fridge, a Tidgy Fridge keeps milk and cola pleasantly cold.

7-27. Another company with superb technical advice is Ryder which supplied the split charged circuitry for the leisure battery and for the second socket on the towing gear.

Ring Automotive, Gelderd Road, Leeds,
LS12 6NB
Tel: 0113 276 7676.
www.ring.ltd.uk

Ryder Towing Equipment Ltd, Mancunian
Way, Ardwick, Manchester, M12 6HJ

Tel: 0161 273 5619
www.rydertowing.co.uk

**Scorpion Vehicle Security Systems
Ltd**, Siemens Road, Northbank Industrial
Estate, Irlam, Manchester, M44 5AH
Tel: 0161 777 9666

7-28. Scorpion can supply and fit Category 1 and Category 2 alarms capable of protecting the external doors, the internal space and the additional space at the rear of a camper not normally covered by a standard car alarm. You can also arm the exterior of the vehicle while leaving the interior clear if you need to leave your pet inside the vehicle.

7-32. Wurth also sells many specialist products, such as this battery terminal spray which eradicates battery 'furring' (as well as corrosion inside components such as light housings), and so helps to keep electrical connections connecting!

7-29. We have been very pleased indeed with the integrated range of Spinflo hob, sink and drainer units. The stainless steel is easy to keep clean and the four-ring hob with grill is more than adequate for a couple's needs.

Spinflo, 4-10 Welland Close, Parkwood Industrial Estate, Rutland Road, Sheffield, S3 9QY
Tel: 0114 273 8157
www.spinflo-group.co.uk

Towsure Ltd, 151-183 Holme Lane, Hillsborough, Sheffield, S6 4JR
Tel: 0114 250 3000
www.towsure.co.uk

Wurth UK Ltd, 1 Centurion Way, Erith, Kent, DA18 4AF
Tel: 08705 987 841
www.wurth.co.uk

For years now, I've been choosing and using Wurth workshop consumables.

Something to do with German vehicle; German quality perhaps? Their products are the best quality I've found but the downside is that you can't often buy them in ordinary retail outlets. You'll have to look in the index in the back of your local *Yellow Pages* for 'Motor factors' for 'trade' outlets, usually tucked away in back streets or on trading estates and almost always more than happy to sell to the public, though it's best to know generally what you want before you go in. Wurth's web site will give you the gen.

7-30. Towsure has a complete range of camping accessories. One of the best we've used is the Caddy Trailer with a lift-up lid. An awning is a really bulky piece of kit but you can get the awning and a lot more besides in the Caddy trailer.

7-31. These rust-prevention materials are an example of the extent of the Wurth range.

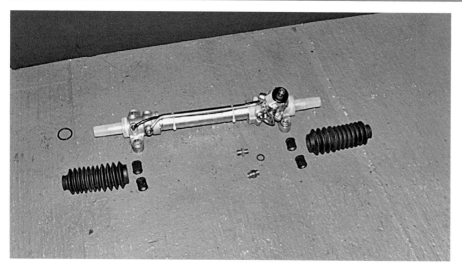

7-33. If you want a power steering rack for your T3 Transporter, I can do no better than recommend ZF, the manufacturer of the racks. The rack will cost you considerably less than buying it through VW and the technical backup that I received was second-to-none.

7-34. This is another classical name in the caravanning world and you will need a Zig mains and 12 volt unit as well as a water level gauge in your camper.

ZF Great Britain Ltd, Abbeyfield Road, Lenton, Nottingham, NG7 2SX
Tel: 0115 986 9211
www.zf-group.co.uk

Zig Electronics Ltd, Units 4, 5 & 10, Phoenix Works, Thrupp, Stroud, Glos, GL5 2BU
Tel: 01453 731 700

Appendix

Clubs & magazines in the UK

We asked each of these clubs and magazines to let you know a bit about themselves. It's well worth joining a club because you can find out where to buy the best parts or accessories, where to go on the best trips, and take advantage of many other benefits.

The Caravan Club, East Grinstead House, East Grinstead, West Sussex, RH19 1UA
Tel: 01342 326 944
www.caravanclub.co.uk

Camping & Caravan Club, Greenfields House, Westwood Way, Coventry, CV4 8JH
Tel: 02476 694 995
www.campingandcaravanningclub.co.uk

Motor Caravanners' Club, 22 Evelyn Close, Twickenham, Middx, TW2 7BN
Tel: 0208 893 3883
www.motorcaravanners.org.uk

The Motor Caravanners' Club provides a focus for over 13,000 active motor caravanners. Since its beginnings in 1960, the Club has become the largest independent owners' club and is run by members for members. Over 25 Local and Special Interest Groups organise in excess of 500 year round events, which all members are invited to attend, with a

minimal of formality, and we are constantly improving services for our members.

Self-Build Motor Caravan Club, 19 Church Street, St Day, Redruth, Cornwall,

7-34. The Caravan Club represents 850,000 caravanners, motor caravanners and trailer tenters. It offers 200 fully-equipped luxury sites as well as 2700 small five-pitch sites in rural situations. The Club also provides a range of quality services for its members including insurance, ferry bookings, overseas site reservations and rescue services. For full details see the Club's web site.

THE CAMPER CONVERSION MANUAL

TR16 5JY
Tel: 01209 821 446
www.sbmcc.fslife.co.uk

Making Motor Caravans Our Way:
The SBMCC was set up to promote and assist those that undertake to build their own Motorcaravan their own way. We are an informal group of people which offers practical help via a very busy online internet forum and have friendly informal meets and weekends away.

If you're embarking on the perilous journey of building one, The Self Build Motor Caravan Club can help you at any stage of your build. The club can be accessed at the address above. Looking forward to hearing from you all.

Type 2 Owners' Club, 57 Humphrey Avenue, Charford, Bromsgrove, B60 3JD

Club 80-90 is a Transporter club which caters just for T3 Transporters. The best way of contacting the 80-90 club is via email on www.club80-90.co.uk

MAGAZINES IN THE UK

Motor Caravan Magazine, IPC Focus Network, Focus House, Dingwall Avenue, Croydon, CR9 2TA
Tel: 0208 774 0737

Motor Caravan Magazine is your one-stop source of practical information, touring tips and vehicle tests. We want you to get the most from your motorhome, and our practical experts can answer all your questions. We're published on the first Friday of each month, and there's more information at www. motorcaravanmagazine.co.uk

Motor Caravanner, 119 Mill Road, Hawley, Dartford, Kent, DA2 7RT
Tel: 01322 272 996
www.motorcaravanner@ukonline.co.uk

Motorcaravan Motorhome Monthly (MMM), Warner Group Publications Ltd, The Maltings, West Street, Bourne, Lincs, PE10 9PH
Tel: 01778 393 313
www.mmmonline.co.uk

MMM is the best-selling and most widely read motorcaravan magazine in the UK: but what makes it unique? *MMM* is the only motorcaravanning magazine to be written and edited by a band of motorcaravanning enthusiasts. Perhaps our motto should

7-35. The Type 2 Owners' Club has a monthly A5 magazine but its main claim to fame is the stunningly successful VanFest meeting which takes place in Malvern, Worcestershire every year. It's got to be the biggest and most enjoyable club event of the year - if not the universe! This aerial photograph of members' T2 Campers was taken to celebrate the T2's birthday.

be, 'By the motorcaravanner; for the motorcaravanner; of the motorcaravanner!' We're traditional in our values, forward-

looking in our ideas, and fair and unbiased in our editorial coverage.

Caravan Motorhome & Camping Mart
Caravan Motorhome & Camping Mart is aimed primarily at buyers and sellers of pre-owned caravans, motorhomes and folding campers. In addition to our ever-growing mart section you will find a comprehensive buyers' guide, news, reviews, plus dealer and manufacturer profiles. Place your classified ad online at www.caravanmart.co.uk for only £10. All this for only £1.75.

Which Motorcaravan, Warner Group Publications Ltd, The Maltings, West Street, Bourne, Lincs, PE10 9PH
Tel: 01778 393 313

Which Motorcaravan is Britain's fastest growing motorhome magazine. Unique in the motorcaravan market, it specialises in vehicle and product testing, with comparison tests of both new and used motorhomes every month. Also included are touring features in the UK and Europe, as well as guides to everything from insurance to motorhome hire.

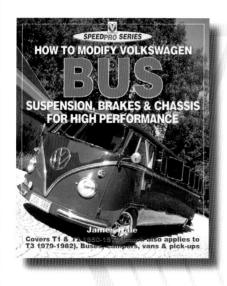
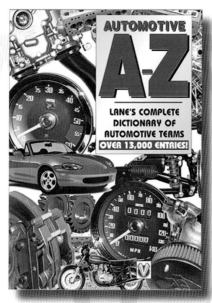
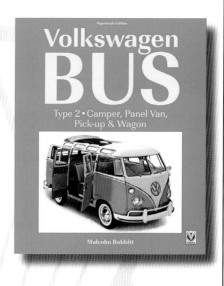
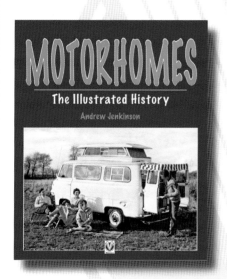
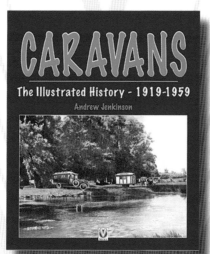
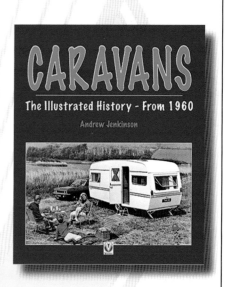

Index